THE
KANSAS CITY BARBEQUE
Society

❖

PRESENTS

Barbeque . . . It's not just for breakfast anymore

A COLLECTION
OF FAVORITE BARBEQUE
RECIPES FROM
THE SOCIETY MEMBERS

This cookbook is a collection of favorite recipes,
which are not necessarily original recipes.

Published by Kansas City Barbeque Society

Copyright© Kansas City Barbeque Society
11514 Hickman Mills Drive
Kansas City, Missouri 64134
1-800-963-KCBS
1-816-765-5891

Library of Congress Catalog Card Number: 95-61897
Hardcover: ISBN: 0-9649176-0-2
Softcover: ISBN: 0-9649176-1-0

Edited, Designed, and Manufactured by
Favorite Recipes® Press
P.O. Box 305142
Nashville, Tennessee 37230
1-800-358-0560

Cover and Book Design: Brad Whitfield
Essayist: Carolyn Wells

Manufactured in the United States of America

First Printing: 1996
Second Printing: 1996
Third Printing: 1998

Contents

Preface

"No man is an island," and this book proves the point. The collective input of more than one hundred contributors makes this a unique barbeque compendium. But, even the finest collective effort still needs direction. Luckily for us, KCBS is filled with talented individuals who willingly gave of their time and expertise to bring this project to completion. Thanks to the following collaborator/compilers for taking this "bull by the horns."

Janeyce Michel-Cupito, Ph.B., Chairperson. Janeyce is head cook of the Powderpuff BBQ team and is a winner of numerous competitions, including two-time winner of the KCBS Spring Training Competition. In "real life," Janeyce is a buyer for the prestigious, Kansas City-based specialty store, Halls. She travels the world searching out the new and innovative in cooking trends. We have been fortunate to have her keen eye and merchandising skill put to use for this cookbook.

Ardie Davis, a.k.a. Remus Powers, Ph.B. Ardie is the founder of the Diddy-Wa-Diddy Barbecue Sauce Contest, now known as the American Royal International Barbecue Sauce Contest. Author of *The Kansas City Barbecue Pocket Guide* and two more barbeque books waiting in the wings, Ardie is an invaluable resource on sauces, restaurants, and regional barbeque. He is manager for the Kansas Department on Aging. His organizational skills and attention to detail have made this work possible, and his humorous writing style has kept the project a pleasure on which to work.

Paul Kirk, K.C. Baron of BBQ, Ph.B., C.W.C., B.S.A.S. (BS Artist Supreme). Paul is one of the most celebrated barbeque chefs in the world. His review, reworking, and standardization of these recipes shaped this into a cogent volume. Paul teaches hands-on barbeque instruction courses around the United States, does barbeque restaurant consulting, and writes for various barbeque newspapers and newsletters. He has won more than 375 ribbons and trophies in competitions, including seven World Championship titles.

Carolyn Wells, Co-founder and Executive Director, KCBS, Ph.B. Carolyn is so wild about barbeque that she spreads the gospel wherever she is and has travelled the world in search of great 'Que. A self-described "foodie," she is a founding member of the Heart of America Chapter of American Institute of Wine & Food (AIWF) and a member of International Association of Culinary Professionals (IACP). In her role as "a serious student of barbeque" she has authored three barbeque books. Her experience and knowledge have proved invaluable to getting this cookbook completed.

Acknowledgments

An organization is only as strong as its membership. The Kansas City Barbeque Society is fortunate to have such a broad-based, dedicated, and enthusiastic group of barbeque devotees who so willingly shared recipes and tricks of the trade. Without them this book would not have been possible.

As the barbeque contest phenomena spread, so did the KCBS network. To the other contest-sanctioning organizations with whom we worked, learned, shared experiences "warts and all," and formed great alliances we say thank you—Memphis in May, International Barbecue Cookers Association, Pacific Northwest BBQ Association, Greater Omaha Barbecue Society, East Texas Barbecue Cookers Association, North Texas Area Barbecue Cookers Association, Central Texas Barbecue Association, and the New England Barbecue Society. All are friends; many are KCBS affiliates.

Many organizations, contest sponsors, and corporations have shared information, sponsored competitions, and fostered the educational experience in the category. We thank the National Pork Producers Council, Missouri and Kansas Pork Producers, National Livestock and Meat Board, The American Royal Association, Lenexa Parks and Recreation, Jack Daniel's, Farmland Foods, MasterFood Specialties, Inc., Oklahoma Joe's, Inc., and the Waylon Company.

The Barbeque trade organizations so graciously cross-promote and enhance involvement in the business of barbeque. We thank the National Barbecue Association and the Barbecue Industry Association. By increasing awareness, barbeque is gaining its rightful title as America's Cuisine.

We thank the authors and publishers who contributed recipes—Jeanne Voltz, Merle Ellis, Leslie Bloom, Park Kerr, Steve Tyler, Chris Schlesinger, Karen Adler and Pig Out Publications Inc., Dr. Rich Davis and Shifra Stein, Bill and Cheryl Alters Jamison, Smoky Hale, Charlie and Ruthie Knote, Jim Auchmuty and Susan Puckett, Paris Permenter and John Bigley, and Vince Staten. Their willingness to share reflects their love of the subject matter. Thanks also to "Coach" Jim Sposato for his 'Que Tips.

To the entrepreneurs and visionaries—those who developed prize-winning sauces, rubs and marinades, cookers, utensils, accessories, fuels, woods, books, tapes, and correspondence courses, we thank you. Because of you, the backyard cooker can barbeque like the professionals. These are not mentioned individually because there are too many to enumerate, but you know who you are.

Finally, to our friends and mentors at Favorite Recipes® Press, we offer great thanks: Dean Tilton, Mary Cummings, Helen Hays, Mary Wilson, artist Brad Whitfield, and most especially to our project leader Debbie Van Mol. Without them this book would still be on the drawing board.

Introduction

Barbeque is a passionate subject. It is the only food group that has a Society, two trade organizations, an annual convention and trade show, seven competition cooking circuits, two newspapers and eight newsletters. It is, after all, the original cooking technique. It is coming into its own in the United States. As best articulated by Mason Steinberg, Old Mill Barbecue, "We've gone through all these ethnic foods, and now, all of a sudden we're discovering our own roots. These roots happen to be barbecue." It is America's Cuisine.

The Kansas City Barbeque Society is the world's largest organization of barbeque enthusiasts. Its members come from all fifty states, most Canadian provinces, and ten foreign countries. They are blue collar workers and professionals. They are men and women. They cross all racial, religious, and socio-economic segments of society. They are competition barbeque cooks and backyarders, whose common denominator is barbeque. They are truly a cultural melting pot.

Barbequers are a generous lot. Because of their passion for barbeque, they are dedicated to promoting their favorite food. They are willing to share their cooking techniques and secrets for great smoked and grilled foods. They are "foodies" who regard their favorite pastime as fun with food. They are the best barbeque cooks in the world. And now, they are ready to share their favorite recipes with you.

If the smell of barbeque sparks a passionate fire in your belly for the taste of real barbeque, this is YOUR book. Keep it at hand, along with your other antidotes for passion. It is user-friendly. It is meant to be used.

As you develop your own great barbeque recipes, we'd love to have you share them with us. Also welcome are techniques, stories, and new products. We will be publishing future editions.

Welcome to the delectable World of Barbeque. We're glad to have you as a part of our family.

What is the Kansas City Barbeque Society?

The Kansas City Barbeque Society (acronym KCBS) is the world's largest organization of barbeque enthusiasts. It is not a radio station or the CBS affiliate in Los Angeles.

KCBS is a nonprofit organization dedicated to "promoting barbeque and having fun while doing so."

KCBS spreads the gospel of barbeque through its newspaper, *The Bullsheet*. This tabloid is full of information on barbeque competitions, upcoming events, personalities, cooking techniques, new products, recipes—all the news that's fit to eat. It is Who's Who and What's Hot in barbeque. *The Bullsheet* is published monthly.

For the computer literate, there's our Barbeque Home Page on the World Wide Web at http://www.barbeque.com. Or you can reach us direct through Compuserve at 75457,312.

KCBS sanctions more than fifty Barbeque Contests across the U.S. each year. It assists civic and charitable organizations in producing these events. The sponsors have a base of cooking teams from which to draw. The cookers know the competition will be fairly officiated according to KCBS Rules and Regulations (which are drawn up by those concerned). The cookers make the rules.

KCBS is a clearinghouse of barbeque information. It networks with barbeque trade organizations and other contest-sanctioning organizations. It tracks trends in barbeque, new products, and equipment. It works with other food organizations to promote barbeque.

Dues are only $20 per year and include a subscription to *The Bullsheet*, a handsome membership certificate, and a window decal. An application to join KCBS can be found at the back of this book.

History of the Kansas City Barbeque Society

It was a dark and stormy night (oops, that's another book).

One evening, in the fall of 1985, Carolyn and Gary Wells and Rick Welch, a.k.a. Sir Loin, were enjoying some friendly libation and chatting about barbeque. Carolyn was Executive Vice-President of Wicker Barbecue Products Company (a great barbeque marinade and baste distributed primarily in the South), and networked extensively in the barbeque market. All competed in the few existing barbeque competitions in the area—The American Royal, The Great Lenexa Barbecue Battle, and the Blue Springs Blaze-Off. Members of other cooking teams were always calling wanting to know when the next event would be held. Sadly, there were none. So, while pondering this dilemma, Carolyn, Gary, and Rick decided to form a club for the cookers. The only criteria for membership was that none of it be taken seriously—to do so was grounds for disqualification. What to name the organization? After semi-serious deliberation, The Kansas City Barbeque Society was deemed to fit the bill. It left a lot of room for interpretation, and there was a fair amount of BS. How to reach these other cookers? We decided to put together a barbeque newsletter. Thus was conceived *The Bullsheet*. Dues were set at $12 per year to cover printing and mailing. About twenty people joined.

Since the first barbeque contest in the area was in late June, the members decided to have an internal contest. In the tradition of baseball, it was dubbed "KCBS Spring Training." Their buddy, Dan Haake, had a horse farm in the country, and agreed to host the event. Having no funds for prize money or trophies, they bought quarter trophies and typed labels for the category prizes. A paper crown was secured for the grand champion. Invitations went out and entries came back. Twenty-two teams entered the first Spring Training, and membership was up to thirty. A good time was had by all, and it was decided that this club was going to be okay.

After the American Royal, in October, there was nothing going on until the next spring. Being in barbeque withdrawal, members decided that they should have a New Year's party in late January (they didn't want to rush into anything). A potluck dinner and brief program was planned. Invitations were sent and more than a hundred people showed up to visit with their barbeque buddies. From the enthusiasm that was building, it was decided that the club be formalized into a real organization. Nine dedicated members were selected for the first Board of Directors. Monthly meetings were held to establish procedures. Periodic newsletters continued to go out, and membership was slightly more than 100.

The Society began receiving calls from organizations wanting to start barbeque competitions. They wanted KCBS to sanction their event. Wait a minute, this is getting serious. Up to this time, each contest had its own set of rules and judging procedures. It was decided to establish a committee to set standard rules and regulations for new contests. A computer literate friend wrote a program for tabulating scores. KCBS was going hi-tech! The contest phenomena was growing rapidly, as was the number of cooking teams and KCBS membership.

The Bullsheet grew from an 8½x11-inch two-sided newsletter to a tabloid. News was expanded from contests only to include all types of barbeque information—personalities, recipes, cooking techniques, and events outside the KC area. There was so much news that the volunteer staff (Carolyn) couldn't get the newsletter out in a timely fashion. The Board decided to hire an editor for *The Bullsheet*. They recruited Bunny Tuttle of the "K-Cass" cooking team. She was short on experience but very long on dedication. The publication further expanded news features. Bunny developed into a first-class editor. It was 1988 and the Society was now up to 800 members.

Calls and letters started coming in from all over the United States. More committees were established to sanction contests, computers were purchased, phone and fax lines added. This thing was taking on a life of its own! Membership continued to grow and the KCBS became an informal information network.

In 1987, Rick Welch, Karen Adler, and Westport Publishers compiled members' recipes into a cookbook called *The Passion of BBQ*. The book sold well in Kansas City and points beyond. It had information about KCBS, so more calls and letters rolled in. The Convention and Visitors Bureau learned of the Society's existence and began referring barbeque inquiries to KCBS. The network was growing.

The tradition of the New Year's Party continued. Programs were added to award a "Team of the Year" based on cumulative contest scores for the previous year. A "Hall of Flame" was initiated. Ribbies (boners) and Piggie (outstanding service) awards were established. Ph.B. (Doctor of Barbeque Philosophy), M.B. (Master of Barbeque), and B.S. (Barbeque Science) degrees were conferred from Remus Powers' Greasehouse University.

By 1993, the KCBS was up to 1,400 members. The systems were in place, and the KCBS ran like a semi-well-oiled machine. The number of contests continued to grow, and KCBS was sanctioning contests in points well beyond the Midwest. Thanks to dedicated members, participation in fund-raising projects allowed the Society to experience further growth. Referral programs increased membership and name recognition.

HISTORY OF THE KANSAS CITY BARBEQUE SOCIETY

In January 1995, the Board participated in strategic planning exercises to determine orderly growth into the next century. Goals and objectives were set, and assignments delegated. Big plans are in the works for the Society, with the emphasis being on barbeque education. Further, expanding the awareness of barbeque from backyard to business is a goal. Still dedicated to promoting barbeque and having fun, KCBS is the voice of the barbeque world.

GETTING
STARTED

Getting Started

Equipment

Pits and Grills: Barbeque grills come in all shapes, sizes, and price ranges. From the $1.99 one-use aluminum "throw away" grill to the $40,000 mobile "big-rig" kitchen, there is no absolute cooking unit. Our advice is to carefully explore the market and invest in the best unit that your wallet will support. A good cooking unit, properly maintained, can last a lifetime. A brief description of the most common follows:

Open Brazier: This unit is fine for grilling steaks, hot dogs, and hamburgers. There is a shallow container for the coals with a grid on top. The hibachi and the $1.99 "throw-away" are examples.

Covered Cooker: This encompasses almost everything else. From the familiar Weber kettle to rectangular or square units with lids, both grilling and barbequing can be achieved. Charcoal and wood chips are the most common fuel.

Kamado Cooker: This is a ceramic, egg-shaped unit with a very tight seal. From a centuries-old Japanese design, these units use very little fuel, and require little tending to the meat. As Dan Maser, distributor of the "Ultimate Cooker" says, "When I sell one of these units, I know it's the last one I'll ever sell to that customer. These cookers have an average life of forty years."

Water Smoker: These units are cylindrical, with a dome-shaped lid. The fire source is in the bottom, and a water pan separates the fire from the meat. They are great for slow smoking. Resist the temptation to peek in on the meat too often.

Gas Grills: The obvious advantage to gas grills is the time required to heat up to cooking temperature. Most commonly used for grilling, it is possible, with practice, to barbeque on a gas grill. Turn off one side, and cook the meat over that part of the grill. The temperature should be low. Smoke flavor can be achieved by using water-soaked wood chips.

Electric Grills: Another quick heating unit, these convenient cookers are great for grilling.

Pellet Smokers: These units are fueled by wood pellets that are automatically fed into the firebox by an auger as the temperature dictates. Used primarily for slow-smoking, there is very little tending to the fire.

Hasty Bake Oven: This "Cadillac" of Outdoor Ovens is well worth the investment. These units can be used for barbequing and grilling, and will soon be introduced as "dual" units—charcoal or gas.

55-Gallon Drum: These units were the forerunner of the custom smokers. In their book *Real Barbecue*, Vince Staten and Greg Johnson give detailed plans on making your own cooker from a 55-gallon drum. Theirs is called "Big Baby."

Custom Smoker: As the barbeque contest phenomenon continues to grow, so does the custom smoker. As competition cooking teams continue to refine their smokers and add enhancements and bells and whistles to give them a cutting edge, an entire new industry has emerged. Many fine metal workers and welding shops will custom fabricate or modify their standard smokers to meet your special needs.

Fuels

Barbeque is usually fueled with charcoal or wood, or a combination of the two. Charcoal alone has little smoke flavor as it has been reduced to carbon (burned in the absence of oxygen). Wood logs, chips, or chunks are tricky to master as a single fuel source for the home cook. But the combination of the two fuel sources is a marriage made in heaven.

Charcoal

Charcoal briquettes may be Henry Ford's second most famous invention. Henry hated waste. He processed the wood scraps from the Model T frames into powdered charcoal, and then compressed them into the now familiar briquette. Henry did us all a great favor. We suspect that he never dreamed of the types of charcoal that would be available a mere seventy years after its inception. Our only caveat is to use a good quality charcoal. Some brands will have too much coal dust as a filler and may leave a nasty flavor on your prized barbeque meats. Charcoal is made from hardwood, and the newest variety is from mesquite. Experiment and see which flavor you like best.

The most commonly used charcoal is the briquette. Briquettes are small pieces of wood or carbon, which have been converted to char (burned in the absence of oxygen). They are ground into powder, mixed with anthracite coal and a starch binder, and compressed into the uniform pillow shape we all know and love. The advantage to using the briquette as a fuel source is that you can easily gauge the way it is going to burn. You can count on even, consistent heat for a reasonably long amount of time. You can raise or lower the heat by using the vents on your closed smoker, closing them to lower the oxygen that fuels the fire, or opening them to increase the temperature.

Available on the market today are "instant-lighting" briquettes. The briquettes or, in some cases, the bag have been impregnated with a petroleum product. Throw on a match, and they all ignite. You'll have ashed-over glowing coals in about twenty minutes, but you may get more than you bargained for, unless you just happen to like the taste of petroleum on your 'Que. Not our favorite fuel.

Recently re-introduced to the charcoal scene is Natural Lump Charcoal. It is what the name implies. It is burned hardwood that is left in its natural state. It is irregular in shape, and is a bit trickier than the familiar briquette. Natural Lump Charcoal burns hotter and cleaner, so you may need to use a bit less.

Finally, there are specialty charcoals. One, manufactured by Hickory Specialties of Brentwood, TN, is charcoal made from used Jack Daniel's white oak whiskey barrels. The whiskey-soaked wood adds a unique taste to barbeque. No, you cannot become intoxicated from eating foods prepared over this fuel. Also, sucking on the briquettes is not recommended.

Another new charcoal is a carbon briquette mixed with unburned wood. It is the fuel (charcoal) and the smoke flavor (unburned wood) all in one.

Woods

The wood of choice in barbequing is usually the one that is most commonly available in your area. The rule of thumb is that any good hardwood will do—experiment and see which you like best with different types of meat. Never, never, never use soft, resinous woods like pine. Likewise, using leftover construction materials or creosote-treated wood to fuel your fire is a no-no. It's nasty beyond words.

Competition barbequers have great debates about which type of wood should be used to smoke which type of meat. A brief description of the most common follows:

Alder: Indigenous to the Pacific Northwest, it makes sense that alder is the wood of choice for smoking fish. The Indian tribes of that area developed alder-smoked salmon into an art form. Modern-day barbequers have adapted the style as their own. Alder has a light delicate smoke that is perfect for fish, and good with any meat.

Apple: Apple has a slightly sweet, fruity smoke that leaves a beautiful pink smoke ring. It's great for poultry and pork. It's almost impossible to over-smoke with fruitwoods, and they will adapt to most all barbeque meats.

Cherry: Like apple wood, cherry is great on most meats—beef, poultry, pork, and game.

Grapevine: Use the vine (not the tendrils) to flavor chicken and fish. It's a light, sweet, delicate smoke.

Hickory: The most commonly used wood for smoking meats. Hickory is great for all types of barbeque, except fish. East of the Mississippi River, hickory is synonymous with barbeque. Restaurants tout their "Real Hickory Smoked Barbeque" in the South. Many competition cookers swear that Shagbark Hickory is the best.

Kiawe: The Hawaiian version of mesquite.

Maple: In Virginia, the maple- and corncob-smoked hams are legendary. This mild smoke works with most meats.

Mesquite: In Texas, ranchers used to pay people to haul away the mesquite scrub. That changed with the discovery that mesquite was great for barbeque. It burns very hot, so is more suited for grilling (mesquite-grilled steak or fish) than smoking. Used as a primary fuel source, it can add an acrid, bitter taste to meats.

Oak: This is the wood of choice in Texas, post oak to be exact. Its mild smoke works for any type of meat, but it especially complements beef.

Peach/Pear: Very versatile as with most fruitwoods.

Pecan: The new "hot" flavor in woods. It is a mild, mellow smoke that works on anything.

Sassafras: Gives a rich color and aroma to red meats.

Aged Wood vs. Green Wood

Green wood burns hotter, longer, and smokier than aged wood.

Logs, Chunks, or Chips?

Logs can be used as a primary fuel source, or combined with charcoal. Logs will burn hot, and require some tending. Obviously, you have to have a cooker large enough to accommodate them, or you'll spend your Saturday chopping wood instead of barbequing.

Chunks are great for barbequing. Soak them in water and add a few to the coals just before you put the meat on the grill. Do not place meat directly over the chunks in case they ignite.

Keep your favorite flavor of chips soaking in a bucket by the grill. Just before putting the meat on, throw a handful of the wet chips on the coals. They will add smoke and moisture to the meat. As you replenish coals, you can throw on more chips.

What if You Have a Gas or Electric Grill and Want Smoke Flavor?

Well, there are a couple of ways you can achieve light smoke on those units. The first is with chips. Soak them in water, then wrap a handful in heavy-duty aluminum foil. Poke holes in the top of the packet to let the smoke escape. Place directly over the lava rock on the gas or electric grill. The heat will cause the wood to smoulder and smoke. When finished cooking (and after the grill has cooled), just remove the packet and discard. Make sure the chips are not smoldering when you dispose of them. No muss, no fuss.

Another way to get smoke in an electric or gas grill is by a smoke can. Envision a small, flat can containing wood pellets. You peel off a sticker that exposes a hole in the top of the can. Place the can directly on the lava rock. It has the same effect as the foil packet above.

There are numerous other gadgets for adding smoke to the cooking chamber. There are cast-iron smoking boxes, aluminum tins filled with chips, etc. Check out your local outdoor living store, and experience ingenuity at work.

Sawdust

Some manufacturers have various flavors of sawdust and smoking "troughs" in their cookers. Sprinkle the dust along the trough and it provides the smoke. Follow the directions of the manufacturer for use.

Pellets

Sawdust Pellets (of many of the wood varieties mentioned above) are used for both primary fuel and smoke source in pellet cookers. The pellets are automatically augered into the firebox as needed. If you like to fiddle (tend the fire, baste the meat, check the temperature) as you cook, this is probably not the unit for you. For easy, almost fool-proof cooking, it's great. The most well-known pellet cooker is the Traeger from Mt. Angel, Oregon.

Lighting the Fire

With gas and electric grills, follow the specific manufacturer's directions for lighting.

There are many fine products available for igniting charcoal. Unfortunately, there are also many that are not so fine.

Absolute Rule #1 for Lighting Charcoal: NEVER, NEVER, NEVER use gasoline to light the fire. Even if you have to delay your barbeque feast by thirty minutes because you have to go to the store and buy a safe charcoal lighter, it's worth it. The barbeque community had this emphasized in 1995 by the loss of veteran barbequer and Memphis pork packer Louis Feinberg, who lost his life in such an accident.

Lighter Fluid: The petroleum-based stuff in cans and squeeze bottles is the most common. They work okay; just be careful not to overdo it. Let the charcoal reach 80% "ash over" before you add meat to the grill. Otherwise, you may get more flavor than you bargained for, with an awful petroleum aftertaste. As you can tell, this is not our starter-of-choice.

Fire Starter Gel: This alcohol-based, ecologically-friendly fire starter is a safe, clean, and easy way to start fires. Put a dollop on the charcoal in several locations, light with match, and away it goes. No giant flame, just a slow-low flame. You can also wash your hands with this gel. After 15 seconds, there will be no trace of the gel and no odor.

Sticks, Strips, Wax Cubes: These are easy to use and clean. Read the directions and product information. Select products that are ecologically friendly and preferably not petroleum based.

Electric Fire Starter: This is a fast, easy, and safe way to ignite charcoal. The only requirement is that you have an electrical outlet close to the grill.

Charcoal Chimney: Commercially available, or make your own (see Equipment section), this is probably the simplest method of lighting charcoal. Crumple paper in the bottom, place charcoal on top, light the paper with a match, and you're on your way. The only inconvenience is moving the coals from the chimney into the grill. The advantage to commercial chimneys is that they have a grate in the bottom and an insulated handle so they are easy to move.

Building the Fire

Generic Method: Make a mound of briquettes (thirty to forty), add fire starter (pick your favorite from page 16), and light coals. Allow to reach 80% ash over; they will have a gray-white ash coating over most of the coals and will be glowing. With small shovel, stick, or long-handled tongs spread coals into desired configuration. For indirect cooking, coals may be banked to one side of the grill (and the meat cooked on the coolest side); or, coals can be spread around the perimeter of the grill and a water pan placed in the middle (meat can be cooked over the water pan).

Replenish with ten to fifteen ashed-over coals every forty-five minutes for slow-smoking.

How Hot is Hot?

Most recipes will call for a hot, medium-hot, medium, or low fire. If you don't have a thermometer, here's an easy way to test the temperature—but do be careful.

Hold your hand, palm side down, just over the grill. Count (using "one thousand one, one thousand two" and so on), until the heat is uncomfortable. If you can keep your hand in place for:

2 seconds—the fire is hot (375-plus degrees)

3 seconds—the fire is medium-hot (350 to 375 degrees)

4 seconds—the fire is medium (300 to 350 degrees)

5 seconds—the fire is low (200 to 300 degrees)

Tools

As with pits and grills, our advice is to invest in the best you can afford. There's nothing worse than pulling your brisket off the smoker and having your tongs collapse! A good set of utensils with wood-insulated handles is well within the reach of most households. What you will need:

Tongs: Use heavy-duty, extra-long, stainless steel tongs with a wood- or plastic-insulated handle. Tongs are great for turning meats; piercing with a fork can lead to loss of juices. You can use another set of tongs to move coals to the cooking unit.

Spatula: Use for turning flat items—fish, hamburgers. Angled spatulas, "Super Flippers," and extra-long-handled spatulas are available.

Spray Bottle: Filled with water to extinguish flare-ups.

Knives: From Ginsus to fine German cutlery, keep your knives sharp. Many needless accidents are caused by dull knives.

Cutting Board: Essential for slicing brisket, cutting ribs, pulling, chopping or shredding pork. Be sure to clean thoroughly after each use. The inexpensive and versatile Chop Chop and the larger Chop Chop Sr. are great for barbequers, and can be washed in the dishwasher.

Instant Read Meat Thermometer: The most under-utilized piece of barbeque equipment, the meat thermometer is the perfect doneness gauge.

Candy Thermometer: A candy thermometer is ideal for placing in a top vent to measure the heat in the cooking unit.

Gloves or Mitts: Heavy-duty gloves allow you to turn/handle meat without overheating the digits. An insulated mitt will achieve the same effect, but lends less dexterity.

Wire Brush: Use this to clean the grill before cooking.

Charcoal Chimney: An ecologically friendly way to start your charcoal. You can buy one for about $15, or make your own. Take a large (empty) coffee can with top and bottom removed. With a jumbo "church key" punch 5 to 6 holes at one end. Rudimentary but functional. Tip: Do not pick up with live coals inside.

Apron: Your favorite slogan, or order one from us. This designer casual wear sets your attire apart from that of the run-of-the-mill backyard cook.

Wok Topper: This is a handy ceramic-coated devise in which to grill small items. Shrimp, mushrooms, vegetables may be stir-fried directly over the hot coals.

Injector: Use to inject marinades into large cuts of meat. Injecting needles are available in gourmet stores.

How to Barbeque, Slow and Low

Barbeque is a cooking technique. It is the slow cooking of meats, usually over an indirect heat source (charcoal and/or wood) at a low temperature (180 to 300 degrees). It requires a covered unit. Barbequing is ideal for large, often poor-quality cuts of meat. After the marriage of the meat, the smoke, and the low, slow heat, a lowly roast or pork shoulder becomes a meal fit for royalty. Barbeque meats may be seasoned or not as the cook sees fit. Purists will insist that no seasoning is necessary for real barbeque. But in the practical world, most barbequers will use their secret blends to complement barbequed meats. See "From The Grill," page 21.

How to Grill, Hot and Fast

Grilling is an excellent way to prepare smaller cuts of meat. It involves cooking meat over direct heat, usually at a high temperature. It's perfect for hot dogs, hamburgers, sausage, steaks and chicken pieces. There's probably not a restaurant in the free world that doesn't have Grilled Chicken Caesar Salad on the menu. Grilled vegetables are gaining great popularity. When grilling, the smoke flavor is minimal. Grilling does not require a closed unit.

Healthy Happy Food
or
How to Lose Weight Without Really Trying

Good food handling habits are, of course, just common sense. Nonetheless, we all fudge a bit here and there, even though we know better. When the gang is gathered 'round the Pit whining to be fed before they pass out from starvation, there is the temptation to break a few rules and bypass normal precautions. But, the next time you're tempted to prepare or serve food without using good healthy preparations, consider this: Would you rather take a little ribbing about being the slowest, cleanest cook in the neighborhood or take a lot of ribbing about your cooking while visiting your guests in the hospital emergency room where they've all gathered? Think about it. Does it really take *that* long to wash your hands after handling raw food or to rinse the cutting board after cutting raw food?

We're providing this primer on basic food safety in the hope that you will take the time to refresh your memory about why this is so important. By following these simple rules you can provide your guests (or the judges at a competition!) with food that will have them clamoring for more rather than turning green at the mention of your name.

The Grill

Always start with a clean grill. (For those of you who still think that the fire will kill off whatever is still stuck to it from the last time you used it: it doesn't!) Scrape the grill with a heavy-duty wire brush, followed with a good dose of soap and hot water. Once the grill is going, don't leave it unattended, especially if there are children in the area. Be sure that your grill is set up on a nonflammable surface and, when all the food has been savored, the leftovers properly stored, and the coals have died away completely, dispose of the ashes.

You and Your Utensils

Wash. Wash. Wash. Wash. It cannot be emphasized enough. The surest way to prevent problems is to wash everything! Start out by washing your hands before touching anything. Then wash again after handling any raw food, and be especially vigilant about washing hands in between handling the various foods you are preparing. Wash all raw meat and vegetables. Wash your cutting board and cutting utensils after finishing each item. To sanitize the board, you can use a mixture of 1 tablespoon of bleach mixed with 1 gallon of water.

To avoid the hazard of cross-contamination, do not use the same bowl or plate to transport meat to the grill and back unless you thoroughly wash and dry it in between.

Storage

Always store meats under proper refrigeration. (This one is especially important for those of you who are competing!) If meat is in a cooler, make sure the temperature is under 40 degrees. Cooked meats should be kept at a minimum of 140 degrees.

For marinades, use a nonreactive dish or a resealable plastic bag. Do not leave marinades standing in the open for long periods. Store in a proper container on the grill or in a cooler. And, don't reuse leftover marinade without first boiling it to kill any food-borne microorganisms.

One final note: Inexpensive latex gloves can be purchased by the box at most full-service drug stores. They're easy to use and we highly recommend them for whenever you're handling meat. Be sure to discard them when you finish with one type of meat and get a fresh pair for the next.

FROM
THE
GRILL

PORK

BARBEQUED WHOLE HOG

Yield: variable

1   whole processed hog   Dry rub to taste
    Vegetable oil

Remove kidneys from hog; rub inside and outside of hog with oil. Coat inside and outside of hog with sweet rub. Wrap feet, tail, head, ears and inside of body cavity with foil; secure foil to inside of body cavity with wooden picks. Place hog in cooker with head toward heat source. Cook at 200° F to 225° F for 10 to 16 hours or until inside meat temperature reaches 170° F on meat thermometer; time depends on size of hog. May use pecan, apple, hickory or oak wood in cooker.

Oklahoma Joe's Owner's Manual & Cookbook

Oklahoma Joe is the founder of the Oklahoma Joe's Interplanetary BBQ Championship in Stillwater, Oklahoma.

"PIG PICKIN" BARBEQUED WHOLE HOG

Yield: variable

1   (90- to 100-pound) whole hog
1   bottle olive oil

1   (to 2) cups barbeque seasoning or rub

Trim excess fat from body cavity; skin inside of rib cage. Rub body cavity with olive oil; season with barbeque seasoning. Cover tenderloins with foil; secure foil with wooden picks or bamboo skewers. Pry hog's mouth open; insert beer or soda can. Cover ears, snout and tail with foil; foil can be removed halfway through cooking process. Place hog in cooker with butt end to heat source. Cook for 12 to 20 hours; time depends on type of cooker used and cooking temperature. Turn hog with head to heat source after 6 to 7 hours. May mop cavity with mop or baste at this time; mopping outside of hog does not affect flavor, but it improves appearance of hog. Remove beer or soda can from hog's mouth before serving and insert apple.

Carolyn Wells

HAPPY "HOLLA" BARBEQUED SMOKED PORK

Yield: 15 servings

¾   cup barbeque sauce
¾   cup honey
1   (4- to 5-pound) bone-in pork loin roast
2   tablespoons extra-virgin olive oil

2   tablespoons Dijon mustard
    Kosher salt to taste
    Freshly ground pepper to taste

Combine barbeque sauce and honey in saucepan. Cook until thickened, stirring frequently. Rub roast with olive oil and Dijon mustard; sprinkle with kosher salt and pepper. Cook roast in smoker at 230° F to 120° F on meat thermometer. Brush roast with barbeque and honey glaze. Cook to 155° F on meat thermometer. Remove from smoker; tent with foil. Let stand for 15 minutes before slicing.

Ed Roith, Happy "Holla" Bar-B-Q

MAPLE-GLAZED PORK LOIN

Yield: 12 servings

1	(3-pound) boneless pork loin	½	cup barbeque sauce
1	teaspoon ground ginger	¼	cup maple syrup
½	teaspoon salt	2	teaspoons grated orange rind

Rub pork loin with mixture of ginger and salt. Insert meat thermometer in thickest part of pork loin. Arrange hot coals around drip pan in covered grill. Place pork loin fat side up on grill rack over drip pan. Grill with lid down for 2 to 2½ hours or to 170° F on meat thermometer. Baste frequently with mixture of barbeque sauce, maple syrup and orange rind during last hour of cooking. Remove to serving platter; cut into thin slices. Garnish with red grapes, green grapes and parsley sprigs.

Bob Zaban, Mr. Z's

Bob Zaban, Mr. Z's, is one of the four winners of the Great American BBQ Roundup. His sauce is now available to the consumer under the BBQ Champs label.

'Que Tip

Fresh pork, like other fresh meats, is naturally low in sodium. Cured pork products such as ham and bacon have a higher sodium content than fresh pork cuts. However, these products are now cured with fifty percent less salt than they were twenty years ago. Today's cured pork products are preserved by refrigeration, not salt.

COUNTRY BOY PORK TENDERLOINS

Yield: 8 servings

1 ½ cups apple butter
1 cup white vinegar
2 ½ tablespoons Worcestershire sauce
2 tablespoons brandy
1 tablespoon soy sauce
1 tablespoon sugar

1 teaspoon dry mustard
1 teaspoon salt
½ teaspoon pepper
½ teaspoon paprika
⅛ teaspoon Tabasco sauce
3 (1-pound) pork tenderloins

Pour mixture of apple butter, vinegar, Worcestershire sauce, brandy, soy sauce, sugar, dry mustard, salt, pepper, paprika and Tabasco sauce over tenderloins in nonreactive dish, turning to coat. Marinate, covered, in refrigerator for 2 to 8 hours, turning occasionally. Drain, reserving marinade. Barbeque pork over semi-direct charcoal fire for 3 hours or until cooked through, turning and basting with reserved marinade every 30 minutes.

Carolyn Wells, author of **Barbecue Greats-Memphis Style**

Country Boy Pork Tenderloins was obtained from Jim Quessenberry of the Arkansas Trav'lers team of Cherry Valley, Arkansas. Jim was the first winner of the Irish Cup in Lisdoonvarna, Ireland.

'Que Tip

The American Heart Association recommends that Americans limit their cholesterol intake to less than 300 milligrams per day. A three-ounce serving of roasted center loin pork contains sixty-six milligrams of cholesterol or twenty-two percent of the recommended maximum.

ROSEMARY GRILLED PORK TENDERLOINS

Yield: 12 servings

1/4 cup red wine vinegar
1/2 cup olive oil
1/2 cup water
2 cloves of garlic, minced
2 tablespoons prepared
   mustard
1 tablespoon salt
1 teaspoon sugar
1/2 teaspoon basil
1/8 teaspoon pepper
2 (1 1/4-pound) pork
   tenderloins

1/4 cup honey
1/4 cup packed brown sugar
1 tablespoon molasses
1 tablespoon prepared
   mustard
1 tablespoon olive oil
1 teaspoon soy sauce
1/4 teaspoon ground ginger
1/2 teaspoon pepper
1 tablespoon fresh
   rosemary leaves

Pour mixture of wine vinegar, 1/2 cup olive oil, water, garlic, 2 table-spoons mustard, salt, sugar, basil and 1/8 teaspoon pepper over pork tenderloins in sealable plastic bag; seal bag. Marinate in refrigerator for 8 hours or longer, turning occasionally. Drain, discarding marinade; pat tenderloins dry with paper towel. Rub mixture of honey, brown sugar, molasses, 1 tablespoon mustard, 1 tablespoon olive oil, soy sauce, ginger and 1/2 teaspoon pepper on all sides of tenderloins; sprinkle with rosemary leaves. Place tenderloins on grill rack over medium-hot coals spiked with wet pecan or mesquite wood chips. Grill for 10 to 15 minutes or until cooked through, turning once. Remove to serving platter; cut each tenderloin into 12 medallions just before serving.

Matt Bilardo

---

*Matt Bilardo markets a mean Green Tomatillo Salsa
packaged under the Bilardo Brothers label.*

BARBEQUED PORK BUTT

Yield: 15 servings

1	(5-pound) pork butt, trimmed	2	teaspoons seasoned salt
3	tablespoons sugar	2	teaspoons celery salt
2	tablespoons paprika	2	teaspoons onion salt
1	tablespoon chili powder	½	teaspoon allspice
1	tablespoon pepper	¼	teaspoon ground cloves
1	tablespoon garlic salt	¼	teaspoon ground ginger
		1	(to 2) cups apple juice

Prepare pork butt as desired. Sprinkle or rub mixture of sugar, paprika, chili powder, pepper, garlic salt, seasoned salt, celery salt, onion salt, allspice, cloves and ginger over pork. Place pork on grill rack in covered grill with water pan. Cook with lid down over medium-low coals for 6 to 8 hours or until cooked through, turning every 1½ hours. Baste with apple juice after 3 hours, at 1 hour intervals.

Geri Reno

CAROLINA-STYLE PORK BUTT

Yield: 20 servings

1	(5-pound) pork butt, boned, rolled, tied	½	cup barbeque seasoning or rub
½	cup prepared mustard	2	cups apple juice

Coat all sides of pork butt with mustard; sprinkle with barbeque seasoning. Place pork on grill rack in covered grill with water pan. Cook with lid down at 230° F to 250° F for 8 to 10 hours or to 170° F on meat thermometer. Turn and baste pork with apple juice every 2 to 3 hours. Remove pork from grill. Let stand for 15 minutes; shred. Serve with buttered buns and coleslaw.

Carolyn Wells

ORANGE-GLAZED PORK BUTT

Yield: 25 servings

½ cup frozen orange juice concentrate	1 teaspoon ground ginger
½ cup honey	1 (5- to 7-pound) pork butt, trimmed
2 tablespoons fresh lime juice	3 tablespoons garlic salt
2 tablespoons butter	1 tablespoon pepper
	1 tablespoon ground ginger

Bring orange juice concentrate, honey, lime juice, butter and 1 teaspoon ginger to a boil in saucepan. Boil for 1 minute. Remove from heat. Sprinkle pork with garlic salt, pepper and remaining 1 tablespoon ginger. Place pork on grill rack in covered grill with water pan. Cook with lid down at 230° F for 7 to 9 hours or to 165° F on meat thermometer. Brush pork with orange glaze 30 minutes before end of cooking process.

Paul Kirk, K.C. Baron of Barbecue

'Que Tip

The word barbeque was coined by French-speaking pirates, who called this Caribbean pork feast "de barbe et queue," which translates "from beard to tail." In other words, the pig roast reflected the fact that the hog was an eminently versatile animal that could be consumed from head to toe.

CHINESE-STYLE BARBEQUED PORK

Yield: 8 servings

¼ cup sweet sherry	1 (2½-pound) boneless
⅓ cup soy sauce	pork rib end roast
1 tablespoon sugar	⅓ cup catsup
1 tablespoon grated fresh	1 tablespoon dry mustard
gingerroot	2 (to 3) teaspoons water
1 clove of garlic, minced	

Pour mixture of sherry, soy sauce, sugar, gingerroot and garlic over roast in nonreactive dish or sealable plastic bag, turning to coat. Marinate, covered, in refrigerator for 8 hours or longer, turning occasionally. Drain, reserving marinade. Place pork on grill rack 6 to 8 inches above drip pan surrounded by hot coals or with coals pushed to back of grill. Brush pork with reserved marinade. Grill for 1 to 1½ hours or to 160° F on meat thermometer, turning and basting with reserved marinade frequently. Stir catsup into remaining marinade. Brush over pork just before end of cooking process. Turn and glaze pork over drip pan. Remove pork to serving platter; tent with foil. Let stand for 30 minutes. Cut into thin slices. Serve with mixture of dry mustard and water. Bring remaining reserved marinade to a boil in saucepan and serve with pork; may swirl mustard sauce into marinade.

Jeanne Voltz, **Barbecued Ribs, Smoked Butts and Other Great Feeds**

'Que Tip

Marinating tenderizes and adds flavor to meat.
When marinating, turn meat occasionally to distribute the
marinade. Use a noncorrosive container such as glass,
porcelain, glazed earthenware, or a sealable plastic bag.

SHERRY-GLAZED RIBS

Yield: 4 servings

1 (8-ounce) can tomato sauce	1 teaspoon granulated onion
1 cup sherry	2 pounds country-style ribs, trimmed
½ cup honey	
2 tablespoons white vinegar	¼ cup salad oil
1 tablespoon Worcestershire sauce	2 tablespoons garlic salt
	1 tablespoon pepper

Bring tomato sauce, sherry, honey, vinegar, Worcestershire sauce and granulated onion to a boil in saucepan over medium heat; reduce heat. Simmer for 10 to 15 minutes or until of glaze consistency, stirring occasionally. Rub both sides of ribs with oil; sprinkle with garlic salt and pepper. Cook ribs with lid down over medium-low coals for 35 to 40 minutes. Turn ribs. Cook with lid down for 30 to 35 minutes longer. Brush ribs with sherry glaze; turn. Cook with lid down for 10 to 15 minutes or until cooked through. Brush both sides with sherry glaze.

Ardie Davis

---

*Ardie Davis, a.k.a. Remus Powers, Ph.B., is author of **The KC BBQ Pocket Guide** published by Pig Out Publications, Inc.*

'Que Tip

Tenderize ribs by piercing both sides between
bones with fork before sprinkling with desired seasonings.
The ribs are done when the meat starts to
pull away from the bone.

BARBEQUED BABY BACK RIBS

Yield: 6 servings

3	(2-pound) racks of pork loin ribs, trimmed	1	teaspoon sage	
3	tablespoons garlic salt	½	teaspoon ground celery seeds	
2	tablespoons paprika	¼	teaspoon cayenne	
1	tablespoon onion salt	1	(to 2) cups apple juice	

Trim excess fat from ribs; remove membrane from back of each rack. Sprinkle both sides of ribs with mixture of garlic salt, paprika, onion salt, sage, celery seeds and cayenne. Place ribs on grill rack in covered grill with water pan. Cook with lid down over medium-hot coals for 4 hours, turning after 1½ hours. Baste every hour with apple juice.

Paul Kirk, K.C. Baron of Barbecue

RIB RUSSELLER RIBS

Yield: 10 servings

5	(2-pound) slabs pork baby back ribs		Red pepper and white pepper to taste
	Salt to taste		Garlic powder to taste
	Paprika to taste	1	(to 2) cups apple juice
	Morton Nature's Seasons Seasoning Blend to taste		

Sprinkle both sides of ribs with mixture of salt, paprika, Morton Nature's seasoning, red pepper, white pepper and garlic powder; wrap in foil. Marinate in refrigerator for 8 hours or longer; discard foil. Cook in smoker at 225° F for 5 hours, spraying with apple juice occasionally.

Skip Russell, Rib Russellers

Skip Russell of the Rib Russellers earned Pork Champion at the American Royal Barbecue Contest, but his "moon over the Royal" may have earned him more recognition!

BARBEQUED SPARERIBS
Yield: 6 servings

1	medium onion, chopped	1	cup tomato sauce
1/3	cup vegetable oil	2	cups beef broth
6	dried red New Mexican chiles, stems removed	1/3	cup cider vinegar
		2	tablespoons dry mustard
6	dried Chiltepins or other small hot chiles	2	tablespoons brown sugar
		3	pounds pork spareribs

Sauté onion in oil in skillet until tender. Add chiles. Sauté until tender. Process onion mixture in blender until puréed. Return puréed mixture to skillet. Add tomato sauce, broth, vinegar, dry mustard and brown sugar; mix well. Bring to a boil; reduce heat. Simmer until thickened, stirring frequently. Grill spareribs 6 inches above hot coals for 30 to 45 minutes or until brown; baste with tomato sauce mixture. Grill for 30 minutes longer, basting with tomato sauce mixture every 5 minutes. May omit Chiltepins to reduce heat.

Chile Pepper

---

*The **Chile Pepper** magazine will send a complimentary issue to interested persons. Call (800) 359-1483.*

BLUE RIBBON RIBS
Yield: 2 servings

1	(2-pound) slab pork ribs, trimmed	Barbeque seasoning to taste

Remove membrane from backside of ribs. Rub both sides of ribs with barbeque seasoning; shake off excess. Cook in smoker at 225° F for 6 to 8 hours or until cooked through.

Guy Simpson

Guy Simpson, KC Rib Doctor, turned his love of barbeque into a successful BBQ spice marketing and catering business.

SMOKED BABY BACK RIBS

Yield: 2 servings

1	(2-pound) slab pork baby back ribs	2	tablespoons sugar
2	tablespoons melted butter	¼	teaspoon salt
		¼	teaspoon pepper

Strip membrane from bone side of ribs. Start fire in water smoker, with water pan filled, and let it reach it's hottest point. Heat for approximately 30 minutes. Add a generous amount of hickory chips to fire for a high degree of smoke. Place ribs bone side down on grill rack. Cook with lid down with heavy smoke for 40 minutes, adding additional hickory chips as needed to maintain high degree of smoke. Remove ribs. Lay on large piece of heavy-duty foil. Brush with mixture of butter, sugar, salt and pepper; seal tightly. Place slab on grill rack. Cook at 180° F to 200° F for 3 hours or until cooked through. Remove slab from grill; cut into individual ribs. Serve with barbeque sauce.

Bill Simon, Three Alarm Smokers

HICKORY-FLAVORED SPARERIBS

Yield: 6 servings

1	(3-pound) slab pork spareribs	½	cup white wine
2	tablespoons onion juice	2	tablespoons water
2	cloves of garlic, crushed	2	tablespoons catsup
1	teaspoon curry powder	½	teaspoon ground ginger
1	tablespoon charcoal salt	⅛	teaspoon rosemary
		⅛	teaspoon pepper

Trim excess fat from spareribs; remove membrane. Mix onion juice, garlic and curry powder in bowl until of paste consistency. Spread over spareribs; sprinkle with charcoal salt. Place in nonreactive dish. Marinate, covered, in refrigerator for several hours. Bring remaining ingredients to a boil in saucepan; reduce heat. Simmer for 5 minutes. Grill spareribs over medium-low coals for 1½ hours or until cooked through, turning and basting with wine sauce frequently.

Ardie Davis

MARINATED BARBEQUED SPARERIBS

Yield: 8 servings

6	(to 7) pounds pork spareribs or 2 slabs	2	tablespoons German coarse ground mustard
1	cup chili sauce	1	tablespoon balsamic vinegar
½	cup fresh lime juice		
¼	cup fresh lemon juice	2	teaspoons grated gingerroot
¼	cup soy sauce		
¼	cup catsup		

Arrange spareribs meat side up on plastic wrap. Spread with mixture of chili sauce, lime juice, lemon juice, soy sauce, catsup, mustard, balsamic vinegar and gingerroot. Pierce meat between each rib with small knife, allowing sauce to penetrate. Wrap securely. Marinate in refrigerator for 8 hours or longer. Unwrap spareribs; scrape excess marinade into bowl. Arrange spareribs meat side up on grill rack. Grill over medium-hot coals for 1¼ hours or until cooked through, turning and basting with marinade every 15 minutes.

Carolyn Wells

'Que Tip

Fresh herbs such as bay leaves, marjoram, rosemary,
thyme, oregano, and sage may be moistened with
water and sprinkled over hot coals to impart additional
flavors to meats and vegetables.

POLYNESIAN SPARERIBS

Yield: 4 servings

1	(3-pound) slab pork spareribs	¼	cup soy sauce
1	cup chicken bouillon	¼	cup catsup
¼	cup honey	2	cloves of garlic, crushed
		2	teaspoons seasoned salt

Trim ribs; cut into halves or into serving portions. Arrange spareribs in nonreactive dish. Pour mixture of bouillon, honey, soy sauce, catsup, garlic and seasoned salt over spareribs, turning to coat. Marinate, covered, in refrigerator for 2 to 3 hours, turning occasionally. Drain, reserving marinade. Grill spareribs with lid down over medium-hot coals for 20 to 30 minutes. Turn spareribs. Cook for 20 to 30 minutes longer. Turn spareribs. Grill for 15 minutes. Turn spareribs. Cook for 15 minutes or until cooked through. Baste with reserved marinade during cooking process.

Ardie Davis

TRES COLINAS RANCH CHINESE BARBEQUED SPARERIBS

Yield: 4 servings

½	cup hoisin sauce	3	cloves of garlic, minced
½	cup soy sauce	2	slabs pork spareribs, trimmed, cut into halves
½	cup catsup		
¼	cup sherry		

Pour mixture of hoisin sauce, soy sauce, catsup, sherry and garlic over spareribs in sealable plastic bag; seal. Marinate in refrigerator for 2 hours, turning occasionally. Drain, discarding marinade. Grill spareribs over medium-hot coals for 45 minutes or until cooked through, turning frequently. May purchase hoisin sauce in Oriental section of grocery store.

Howard Smith

APPLE-SMOKED PORK CHOPS

Yield: 6 servings

1	(15-ounce) can applesauce	1	teaspoon garlic powder
¼	cup lemon juice	1	teaspoon seasoned pepper
2	tablespoons honey	6	(6-ounce) pork chops

Pour mixture of applesauce, lemon juice, honey, garlic powder and seasoned pepper over pork chops in sealable plastic bag; seal. Marinate in refrigerator for 2 to 4 hours, turning occasionally. Drain, reserving marinade. Grill pork chops over medium-hot coals until cooked through, turning and basting with reserved marinade frequently.

Ernie Heimsoth

ST. LOUIS PORK STEAKS

Yield: 6 servings

6	(6-ounce) pork steaks, ½-inch thick	1	tablespoon celery salt
		1	tablespoon pepper
2	tablespoons garlic salt	2	cups barbeque sauce

Sprinkle both sides of steaks with garlic salt, celery salt and pepper. Grill over medium-hot coals until cooked through, turning frequently. Brush barbeque sauce liberally on steaks; turn. Grill for several minutes. Repeat process until all barbeque sauce is used. Be careful not to caramelize or burn sauce.

Carolyn Wells

Carolyn Wells credits this recipe to John Lillich of the Lazy L Smokers. John was one of the original KCBS board members and the first membership chairperson.

APPLE-GLAZED PORK KABOBS

Yield: 6 servings

1	cup apple jelly	1	tablespoon garlic salt
2	tablespoons honey	2	teaspoons celery salt
2	tablespoons lemon juice	1	teaspoon pepper
2	tablespoons unsalted butter	1	large onion, cut into 1-inch pieces
1	teaspoon cinnamon	2	large green bell peppers, cut into 1-inch pieces
¼	teaspoon ground cloves	½	cup olive oil
1	pound pork loin, cut into 1-inch cubes		

Soak 6 bamboo skewers in water in shallow dish. Combine apple jelly, honey, lemon juice, butter, cinnamon and cloves in saucepan; mix well. Cook over medium heat until jelly melts, stirring frequently; reduce heat. Simmer until of glaze consistency, stirring frequently. Sprinkle pork with garlic salt, celery salt and pepper. Thread pork, onion and green peppers alternately onto bamboo skewers. Place skewers in nonreactive shallow dish. Pour olive oil over kabobs, turning to coat. Grill over medium-hot coals for 12 to 15 minutes or until pork is cooked through and vegetables are tender, turning and basting with apple glaze frequently.

Paul Kirk, K.C. Baron of Barbecue

'Que Tip

Soak wooden or bamboo skewers in water for 30 minutes before using to prevent burning while grilling.

PORK BUTT HASH

Yield: 4 servings

2 medium potatoes, peeled, grated	8 ounces leftover pork butt, cut into cubes
2 tablespoons olive oil	10 drops of Tabasco sauce or to taste
2 medium onions, coarsely chopped	Salt to taste
Pepper to taste	

Squeeze excess moisture from potatoes. Heat olive oil in skillet over medium heat. Add onions; sprinkle with pepper. Sauté for several minutes. Sprinkle ¹/₂ of the grated potatoes evenly over the onions; season with pepper. Repeat the process with remaining potatoes. Turn onions over, using wooden spoon; potatoes should be on bottom. Cook for 10 minutes or just until potatoes and onions are tender, stirring frequently. Stir in pork. Cook just until heated through, stirring occasionally. Season with Tabasco sauce and salt. May substitute vegetable oil for olive oil. May substitute beef brisket for pork butt for Brisket Hash.

Bob Lyon

Bob Lyon of the Beaver Castors is the Pacific Northwest correspondent for **The Bullsheet**, **National Barbecue News** *and the* **Goat Gap Gazette**.

'Que Tip

The grill is easier to clean when it is warm. Use a wire brush or wadded newspaper. Remove the ashes after the grill has cooled. This will prevent corrosion in the bottom of the grill.

BARBEQUED PORK BURGERS

Yield: 6 servings

2 tablespoons vegetable oil	1 teaspoon Worcestershire
1½ pounds ground pork	sauce
½ cup minced green bell	1 teaspoon prepared
pepper	mustard
½ cup catsup	1 teaspoon seasoned salt
¼ cup packed brown sugar	½ teaspoon ground ginger
1 tablespoon minced onion	6 onion buns, split

Heat oil in saucepan over medium heat. Add pork. Sauté until soft, but not brown; drain. Stir in green pepper, catsup, brown sugar, onion, Worcestershire sauce, mustard, seasoned salt and ginger. Shape into 6 patties. Grill over medium-hot coals until cooked through; if flare-ups occur close lid to cooker. Serve on onion buns.

Paul Kirk, K.C. Baron of Barbecue

SPICY PORK BURGERS

Yield: 4 servings

1 pound ground pork	1 teaspoon seasoned salt
¼ cup buttermilk	1 teaspoon pepper
2 tablespoons minced onion	½ teaspoon granulated
1 (to 2) teaspoons sage	garlic
1 teaspoon crushed red	⅛ teaspoon oregano
pepper	

Combine pork, buttermilk, onion, sage, red pepper, seasoned salt, pepper, garlic and oregano in bowl; mix well. Shape into patties. Grill over medium heat for 8 minutes per side.

Paul Kirk, K.C. Baron of Barbecue

POULTRY

~~~~~

BLUE RIBBON CHICKEN

Yield: 4 servings

1 (3½-pound) chicken, whole or cut into pieces	Favorite barbeque rub to taste

Rinse chicken and pat dry. Sprinkle all sides of chicken with barbeque rub 15 minutes before grilling. Grill over medium-hot coals until cooked through or until juices run clear when chicken is pierced with fork. May cook in smoker at 225° F for 3 to 4 hours or until cooked through. Serve with favorite barbeque sauce.

Morgan Olander, Hawg Pen

Morgan Olander, of the Hawg Pen team, is a former Grand Champion of the American Royal Open Barbecue Contest.

FANCY CHICKEN WITH GOAT CHEESE

Yield: 4 servings

1	(3½-pound) chicken	1	cup chicken stock
2	(to 3) ounces mild goat cheese	½	cup white wine
		½	cup water
1	tablespoon pesto	2	tablespoons olive oil
8	(to 10) basil leaves	1	tablespoon pesto

Rinse chicken and pat dry. Massage inside and outside of chicken with goat cheese and 1 tablespoon pesto, working the ingredients as far as possible under the skin without tearing. Insert basil leaves under skin, placing them as evenly as possible over chicken. Truss, if desired. Place chicken in sealable plastic bag. Chill for 8 hours or longer. Remove chicken from bag. Let stand at room temperature for 30 minutes. Heat chicken stock, white wine, water, olive oil and 1 tablespoon pesto in saucepan. Keep warm over low heat. Arrange chicken breast side down on rack in smoker. Cook for 1¾ to 2 hours, basting with warm wine sauce every 30 minutes if using a wood-burning pit or as appropriate for your style of smoker. Turn the chicken breast side up. Cook for 1¾ to 2 hours longer or to 180° F to 185° F on meat thermometer, basting every 30 minutes. Transfer chicken to serving platter. Let stand for 5 to 10 minutes. Remove skin; carve as desired. May omit wine sauce. Serve with pasta tossed with olive oil, steamed zucchini and peach cobbler.

Cheryl Alters Jamison & Bill Jamison, **Smoke & Spice**

'Que Tip

Thaw chicken in the refrigerator or in cold water.
It takes approximately twenty-four hours to thaw a
four-pound chicken in the refrigerator or from three to
nine hours to thaw chicken pieces.

JAMAICAN JERK CHICKEN

Yield: 12 servings

3	(3½- to 4-pound) chickens	2	tablespoons corn oil
4	medium onions, coarsely chopped	2	tablespoons whole allspice berries, crushed
2	cloves of garlic, minced	2	tablespoons crushed red pepper
4	green onions, chopped	1	tablespoon sugar
1¼	cups soy sauce	1	teaspoon nutmeg

Rinse chickens and pat dry. Process onions, garlic and green onions in food processor until coarsely ground. Combine onion mixture with soy sauce, corn oil, allspice, red pepper, sugar and nutmeg in bowl; mix well. Pour over chickens in large sealable plastic bag. Press air from bag; seal. Marinate in refrigerator for 8 hours or longer, turning occasionally. Drain, reserving marinade. Grill over low heat until chickens are brown and juices run clear when chickens are pierced with fork, turning and basting with reserved marinade occasionally.

Bill Robinson, Fire N' Smoke

Bill Robinson is a Kansas City, Kansas, postal worker turned barbeque caterer.

'Que Tip

Baste chickens every thirty to forty-five minutes to prevent drying. Whole chickens are done when the drumstick can be turned easily and removed.

SMOKEMASTERS SMOKED CHICKEN

Yield: 4 servings

1	(3½-pound) chicken	¼	cup barbeque seasoning
½	cup Italian salad dressing	2	cups apple juice
½	cup soy sauce		

Rinse chicken with cold water and pat dry. Mix salad dressing and soy sauce in bowl; strain. Inject chicken breasts, thighs and legs with salad dressing mixture. Sprinkle barbeque seasoning evenly over chicken. Place chicken in sealable plastic bag; seal bag. Marinate in refrigerator for 8 hours or longer. Remove chicken from bag. Cook chicken in smoker at 250° F over indirect heat for 4 hours or until cooked through, misting with apple juice every 30 minutes. Use hickory chips or apple wood in smoker.

Bob Lane, Mozark Smokemasters

Bob Lane of the Mozark Smokemasters won first place in the Poultry division at the Valley Fare Daze in Grain Valley, Missouri, with this recipe.

TARRAGON BUTTER-BARBEQUED CHICKEN

Yield: 8 servings

2	(3-pound) chickens	1	tablespoon Dijon mustard
1	cup butter, softened		
3	shallots, minced	1	tablespoon coarsely ground pepper
2	tablespoons minced fresh tarragon		Seasoned salt to taste

Rinse chickens and pat dry. Combine butter, shallots, tarragon, Dijon mustard and pepper in bowl; mix well. Rub chickens inside and out with some of the butter mixture. Loosen skin carefully from chicken breast; insert remaining butter mixture beneath skin. Sprinkle with seasoned salt. Place chicken on grill rack in covered grill with water pan. Grill with lid down over indirect heat for 3 hours or until juices run clear when chickens are pierced with fork.

Ardie Davis

ORANGE CHICKEN

Yield: 8 servings

2 (3-pound) chickens, cut into halves	½ cup white wine
2 cups orange juice	¼ cup unsalted butter
½ cup packed brown sugar	2 tablespoons garlic salt
	1 tablespoon pepper

Rinse chickens and pat dry. Arrange in nonreactive dish. Combine orange juice, brown sugar, white wine and butter in saucepan. Cook until butter melts, stirring frequently. Pour over chickens, turning to coat. Marinate, covered with plastic wrap, for 2 to 3 hours, turning occasionally. Drain, reserving marinade. Sprinkle chickens with garlic salt and pepper. Place skin side up on grill rack in covered grill. Grill with lid down over medium-hot coals for 1½ hours, turning and basting with reserved marinade every 20 to 30 minutes.

Paul Kirk, K.C. Baron of Barbecue

GRILLED LEMON CHICKEN

Yield: 4 servings

1 (3-pound) chicken, cut into quarters	1 teaspoon liquid smoke
½ cup fresh lemon juice	½ cup finely chopped fresh basil
½ cup light clover honey	½ teaspoon coarsely ground pepper
¼ cup olive oil	
2 cloves of garlic, crushed	

Rinse chicken and pat dry. Remove backbone; flatten breastbone with meat mallet. Arrange in nonreactive dish. Process lemon juice, honey, olive oil, garlic and liquid smoke in food processor for 30 seconds. Stir in basil and pepper. Pour over chicken, turning to coat. Marinate, covered, in refrigerator for 6 hours, turning occasionally. Drain, reserving marinade. Grill chicken 4 to 6 inches above medium-hot coals for 40 minutes or until cooked through, turning and basting with reserved marinade every 10 minutes.

Bill Simon, Three Alarm Smokers

HONEY DIJON BARBEQUED CHICKEN

Yield: 8 servings

2 (3-pound) chickens, cut into quarters	2 tablespoons Dijon mustard
½ cup olive oil	2 cloves of garlic, crushed
½ cup white zinfandel	1 teaspoon pepper
¼ cup clover honey	½ teaspoon salt

Rinse chicken and pat dry. Place chicken quarters in 2 sealable plastic bags. Pour mixture of olive oil, wine, honey, Dijon mustard, garlic, pepper and salt over chicken; seal. Marinate in refrigerator for 2 to 4 hours, turning occasionally. Drain, reserving marinade. Grill chicken with lid down over medium-hot coals for 20 to 30 minutes per side or until cooked through, basting frequently with reserved marinade.

Carolyn Wells

CAROLINA MUSTARD CHICKEN

Yield: 8 servings

¼ cup vegetable oil	1½ cups seasoned chicken broth
8 chicken breast halves	¼ cup Dijon mustard

Pour oil into saucepan that can be used on grill. Rinse chicken and pat dry. Arrange chicken on grill rack 4 inches above medium-hot coals; brush with some of the oil. Grill until brown. Turn chicken; brush with some of the oil. Grill until brown. Stir chicken broth and Dijon mustard into remaining oil. Heat at edge of grill. Brush chicken generously with mustard mixture. Grill for 30 to 45 minutes or until cooked through, turning and basting with mustard mixture as needed. Reheat remaining mustard sauce and serve with chicken. May substitute thighs or legs for chicken breasts. May substitute butter for vegetable oil.

Jeanne Voltz, **Barbecued Ribs, Smoked Butts and Other Great Feeds**

HERB-SMOKED CHICKEN

Yield: 4 servings

4	chicken breast halves	2	teaspoons minced fresh parsley
¼	cup vegetable oil	1	teaspoon celery powder
¼	cup olive oil	½	teaspoon rosemary
½	cup sauterne	½	teaspoon tarragon
½	cup chicken broth	½	teaspoon pepper
6	tablespoons apple jelly, melted	½	cup white wine Worcestershire sauce
3	tablespoons lemon juice	½	cup honey
1	tablespoon Worcestershire sauce	¼	cup melted margarine
2	teaspoons seasoned salt	½	teaspoon garlic salt

Rinse chicken and pat dry. Arrange chicken in nonreactive dish. Pour mixture of vegetable oil, olive oil, wine, broth, apple jelly, lemon juice, 1 tablespoon Worcestershire sauce, seasoned salt, parsley, celery powder, rosemary, tarragon and pepper over chicken, turning to coat. Marinate, covered, in refrigerator for 3 to 8 hours or longer, turning occasionally. Drain, reserving marinade. Cook chicken in water smoker at 200° F using apple wood for 3½ hours or until cooked through, basting with reserved marinade every 30 minutes. Glaze chicken with mixture of ½ cup white wine Worcestershire sauce, honey, margarine and garlic salt 20 minutes before end of cooking process. Reduce cooking time to 1¾ hours and baste and turn chicken every 15 to 20 minutes if using smoker without water pan.

Keith Lindblom, Holy Smokers

---

*Keith Lindblom of the Holy Smokers won a ribbon in Poultry
at the American Royal Barbecue Contest.*

TEQUILA CHICKEN

Yield: 6 servings

6 boneless skinless chicken breast halves
1 cup chicken broth
½ cup olive oil
½ cup tequila
¼ cup minced green onions
3 cloves of garlic, crushed
3 tablespoons fresh lime juice
1 tablespoon chili powder
1 tablespoon minced cilantro
1 teaspoon salt
1 teaspoon cumin
½ teaspoon coriander

Rinse chicken and pat dry. Arrange in shallow nonreactive dish. Pour mixture of broth, olive oil, tequila, green onions, garlic, lime juice, chili powder, cilantro, salt, cumin and coriander over chicken, turning to coat. Marinate, covered with plastic wrap, in refrigerator for 2 to 3 hours, turning occasionally. Drain, discarding marinade. Grill chicken over medium-hot coals for 4 to 5 minutes per side or until cooked through. Arrange on serving platter. Garnish with lime wedges.

Paul Kirk, K.C. Baron of Barbecue

'Que Tip

Arrange chicken skin side up on grill rack with
smaller pieces near the edges.

WILDCAT CHICKEN

Yield: 4 servings

4	boneless skinless chicken breast halves	3	tablespoons Dijon mustard
2	tablespoons sugar	½	teaspoon Tabasco sauce
½	cup soy sauce	¼	teaspoon Worcestershire sauce
1	cup mirin (sweetened Japanese rice wine)	1	tablespoon toasted sesame seeds
2	tablespoons rice vinegar	4	sesame seed hamburger buns, split
5	tablespoons mayonnaise		

Rinse chicken and pat dry. Bring sugar, soy sauce, mirin and rice vinegar to a boil in saucepan. Boil for 8 to 10 minutes or until reduced to ³/₄ cup, stirring occasionally. Keep glaze warm over low heat. Whisk mayonnaise, Dijon mustard, Tabasco sauce and Worcestershire sauce together in bowl until blended; adjust seasonings. Set aside. Arrange chicken on grill rack brushed with oil. Grill with lid down over moderately hot coals for 3 minutes per side to sear. Grill for 6 to 8 minutes longer or until cooked through, turning and basting with warm glaze every 2 minutes. Sprinkle with sesame seeds. Remove to warm platter. Toast cut side of buns on grill. Spread mayonnaise mixture on cut sides of buns. Place chicken on bottom halves of buns; top with remaining buns. Serve with sliced cucumbers and tomatoes drizzled with basil vinaigrette and steamed corn on the cob. May substitute honey mustard or mustard with seeds for Dijon mustard. Mirin and rice vinegar are available in Oriental grocery stores, gourmet grocery stores and in the specialty section of most supermarkets. May omit sesame seeds.

Leslie Beal Bloom, **Chicken on the Run**

BARBEQUED CHICKEN

Yield: 8 servings

2 (3½-pound) chickens	1 teaspoon salt
1½ cups tomato juice	1 teaspoon cumin
¼ cup chopped onion	½ teaspoon garlic powder
2 tablespoons lemon juice	¼ teaspoon lemon pepper
2 tablespoons Worcestershire sauce	¼ teaspoon hot pepper sauce

Rinse chickens and pat dry. Cut into pieces. Pour mixture of tomato juice, onion, lemon juice, Worcestershire sauce, salt, cumin, garlic powder, lemon pepper and hot pepper sauce over chicken in sealable plastic bag; seal. Marinate in refrigerator for 12 hours, turning occasionally. Drain, reserving marinade. Arrange chicken, with no pieces touching, on grill rack in covered grill with water pan. Grill with lid down over indirect heat for 1 hour; baste with reserved marinade. Turn chicken. Grill for 1 to 1½ hours longer or until cooked through.

Bill Simon, Three Alarm Smokers

HONEY-GLAZED CHICKEN

Yield: 6 servings

4 pounds chicken pieces	2 tablespoons butter or margarine
¼ cup honey	
3 tablespoons prepared mustard	1 tablespoon Worcestershire sauce

Rinse chicken and pat dry. Heat honey, mustard, butter and Worcestershire sauce in saucepan until blended, stirring occasionally. Arrange dark meat chicken on grill; cover. Grill over medium-hot coals for 15 minutes, turning once. Add white meat chicken to grill. Grill for 15 to 20 minutes longer or until cooked through, turning occasionally. Baste with honey mixture during last 10 minutes of cooking process.

Donna McClure, P.D.T. (Pretty Damn Tasty)

CUZIN HOMER'S CHICKEN DELIGHTS

Yield: 12 servings

12 chicken thighs, skinned, boned	12 slices thinly sliced smoked bacon
1 envelope ranch salad dressing mix	1½ (to 2) cups barbeque sauce
2 pickled jalapeños, cut into 12 thin slivers	

Rinse chicken and pat dry. Coat chicken with salad dressing mix. Make 1 slit with sharp knife in each thigh; insert 1 jalapeño sliver into each slit. Wrap each thigh with 1 slice of bacon; secure with wooden pick. Arrange in nonreactive dish. Pour barbeque sauce over chicken, turning to coat. Marinate, covered, in refrigerator for 1 hour or longer, turning occasionally. Arrange chicken on grill rack in covered grill. Grill over medium-hot coals until bacon is crisp. Smoke with lid down until chicken is cooked through, turning occasionally. May glaze with additional barbeque sauce if desired.

John Raven

John Raven, the Commissioner of BBQ, submitted this recipe. It was developed by Cuzin Homer Page, one of the top ten barbequers in the state of Texas.

'Que Tip

A three-and-one-half-pound chicken serves four people and yields approximately three cups of chopped cooked chicken.

ORIENTAL BURGERS

Yield: 4 servings

8	ounces boneless skinless chicken breasts	1	teaspoon rice wine or sherry
4	dried shiitake mushrooms, stems removed	1	teaspoon sesame oil
½	teaspoon freshly ground black pepper	1	tablespoon soy sauce
1	(½-inch piece) gingerroot, chopped	¼	(to ½) teaspoon chile paste or crushed red pepper flakes
1	carrot, peeled, cut into eighths	3	tablespoons dry Japanese bread crumbs or fine bread crumbs
2	green onions, cut into quarters	4	sesame seed hamburger buns, toasted

Rinse chicken and pat dry; cut into 1-inch pieces. Soak mushrooms in enough hot water to cover in bowl for 15 minutes; weight mushrooms to immerse completely. Drain and squeeze excess liquid from caps. Cut mushrooms into halves. Process gingerroot in food processor until minced. Add mushrooms, carrot and green onions. Process until minced, scraping bowl as needed. Add chicken. Process with on/off turns to coarsely chop. Stir in mixture of rice wine, sesame oil, soy sauce, chile paste and black pepper and bread crumbs. Shape into 4 patties. Arrange patties on grill rack brushed with oil in covered grill. Grill over hot coals for 4 minutes per side. Cook for 5 minutes longer, turning once. Serve on toasted buns. May broil for 10 minutes, turning 3 times. May substitute fresh shiitake mushrooms for dried shiitake mushrooms. May substitute chicken thighs for chicken breasts. Shiitake mushrooms and rice wine are available in Oriental grocery stores, gourmet grocery stores and in most supermarkets.

Leslie Beal Bloom, **Chicken on the Run**

SMOKED RED CHILE-RUBBED CORNISH HENS

Yield: 8 servings

4	chunks mesquite smoking wood	¼	cup olive oil
4	(1¾-pound) Cornish game hens	8	teaspoons mild chili powder blend

Soak wood in water to cover in large container for 2 hours. Place water smoker outdoors in location shielded from the wind. Rinse game hens and pat dry. Remove excess fat from body cavities; tie legs together with kitchen twine. Rub each game hen with 1 tablespoon of the olive oil. Sprinkle each with 2 teaspoons of the chili powder blend; rub firmly into skin. Drain wood chunks. Place in smoker and set basin of water in place according to smoker manufacturer's directions. Arrange game hens on lower rack of smoker. Smoke with lid down for 2½ hours or until juices run clear when thigh is pierced with fork. Cool slightly on rack. Cut game hens lengthwise into halves. Arrange on serving platter.

W. Park Kerr, **Texas Border Cookbook**

Park, and his mom, Norma, are owners of the El Paso Chile Co.

'Que Tip

Always wash hands, countertops, cutting boards, knives, and other utensils used in preparing raw chicken before they come in contact with other raw or cooked foods.

SMOKED TURKEY

Yield: 10 servings

1	(10- to 12-pound) turkey	1	medium onion, cut into wedges
	Lemon pepper to taste		
1	apple, cut into wedges	½	cup orange juice
1	orange, cut into wedges	1	cup water

Rinse turkey and pat dry. Remove neck and giblets; discard. Sprinkle inside of body cavity with lemon pepper; place apple, orange and onion wedges inside body cavity. Cook turkey in kettle over drip pan over indirect heat, using alder wood. Pour orange juice and water in drip pan. Place 3 chunks of alder wood on each side of charcoal. Place turkey on grill rack over drip pan. Cook for 3 to 3½ hours or until cooked through. Add additional charcoal and alder wood as needed.

C. E. "Ol' Smokey" Tuttle, Chips Off Ol' Smokey

C. E. "Ol' Smokey" Tuttle has four sons, all of whom are now involved in competition barbequing.

'Que Tip

If using a meat thermometer when grilling chicken, let the internal temperature reach 180° F for whole chicken, 170° F for bone-in pieces, and 160° F for boneless pieces.

TURKEY MEATBALLS

Yield: 6 servings

12	ounces ground turkey	2	tablespoons vegetable oil
½	cup fresh bread crumbs	1	cup chopped onion
¼	cup grated Parmesan cheese	4	ounces mushrooms, sliced
1	egg, beaten	1	large green bell pepper, chopped
¼	cup chicken broth	1	tablespoon chopped garlic
⅛	teaspoon nutmeg	2	cups crushed canned tomatoes
⅛	teaspoon cumin		
1	teaspoon chopped garlic	½	cup dry white wine
4	teaspoons chopped fresh parsley	1	teaspoon rosemary
	Salt and pepper to taste	1	bay leaf
1	pound sweet or hot Italian sausage, cut into bite-size pieces	¼	cup chopped fresh basil

Combine ground turkey, bread crumbs, cheese, egg, broth, nutmeg, cumin, 1 teaspoon garlic, parsley, salt and pepper in bowl; mix well. Shape into balls. Cook turkey balls and sausage in oil in nonstick skillet for 10 minutes or until brown on all sides; drain. Sprinkle onion, mushrooms, green pepper and 1 tablespoon garlic around meatballs. Cook for 3 minutes, stirring constantly. Add tomatoes, white wine, rosemary and bay leaf; mix well. Stir, scraping bottom of pan to loosen browned particles. Cook, covered, for 10 minutes, stirring occasionally. Discard bay leaf; sprinkle with basil. Serve over hot cooked penne, ziti or rice.

Trip Mason, Trip Mason and the Ciambatta Racing Team

BEEF

~~~

BARBEQUED BRISKET

Yield: 30 servings

1   (9- to 10-pound) beef
    brisket
1   cup mustard sauce

1   cup barbeque seasoning
    or rub

Trim brisket fat to ⅛ to ¼ inch; trim fat pockets flush with side of brisket. Coat fat side with some of the mustard sauce; sprinkle with some of the barbeque seasoning. Turn brisket. Repeat procedure with remaining mustard sauce and barbeque seasoning. Place brisket fat side up on grill rack in covered medium grill with a water pan. Arrange brisket with large end to the heat source. Cook at 230° F to 250° F over indirect heat for 8 to 12 hours. Turn and mop brisket after 4 to 6 hours; rotate blade portion to heat. Turn and mop every 1½ hours until cooked through. Brisket is done when you can insert a probe into the meat easily and remove without any resistance.

Carolyn Wells

Carolyn Wells no longer competes in barbeque contests. Her husband Gary officiated at her last competition in Grain Valley, Missouri. The teams were suspicious when she earned two first-place trophies, but she also came in dead-last in two categories!

BARBEQUED BEEF & ONION PIZZA

Yield: 8 servings

1	(16-ounce) loaf frozen bread dough	1	tablespoon butter, softened
3	tablespoons melted butter	2	teaspoons olive oil
3/4	cup sweet smoke-flavor barbeque sauce	8	ounces smoked beef brisket, cut into bite-size pieces
3/4	teaspoon beef concentrate		
1	large onion, thinly sliced, separated into rings	1 1/2	cups shredded provolone cheese
1/4	cup water		

Thaw bread dough using package directions. Let rise until doubled in bulk. Combine 3 tablespoons butter, barbeque sauce and beef concentrate in bowl; mix well. Combine onion rings, water and 1/4 cup of the butter sauce in heavy skillet. Cook, partially covered, over high heat until onion is tender and lightly caramelized. Grease 10x15-inch baking pan with mixture of 1 tablespoon butter and olive oil. Pat bread dough over side and bottom of prepared pan; spread with 1/2 cup of the remaining butter sauce. Bake at 500° F for 5 minutes. Remove from oven. Arrange brisket over baked layer; drizzle with remaining butter sauce. Top with onion rings. Bake at 475° F for 6 minutes longer or until edges are light brown. Sprinkle with cheese. Broil until cheese is brown and bubbly.

Art Siemering

Art Siemering is a nationally recognized food writer. His newsletter, **Trend/Wire,** *tracks the latest trends in the industry.*

'Que Tip

Fill fajitas, tacos, burritos, or enchiladas
with sliced or chopped brisket.

FAUX FAJITAS

Yield: 24 servings

1 (4-pound) smoked beef brisket, sliced into ⅛x½-inch strips
1 (to 2) cups barbeque sauce
24 flour tortillas, heated
2 (16-ounce) cans refried beans, heated
1½ (to 2) cups guacamole
1 large onion, chopped
2 (16-ounce) jars hot salsa

Cover brisket with just enough barbeque sauce to coat in large skillet. Cook, covered, over low heat just until heated through. Spread warm tortilla with thin layer of beans. Top with brisket, guacamole, onion and salsa; roll to enclose filling. Repeat process with remaining tortillas.

John Raven

JALAPENO BRISKET

Yield: 30 servings

1 (10-ounce) jar sliced jalapeños
1 (6- to 10-pound) beef brisket, trimmed
Garlic salt to taste
Pepper to taste
2 large purple onions, sliced

Drain jalapeños, reserving liquid. Pierce each side of brisket with fork or knife 40 to 50 times. Pour reserved jalapeño liquid over both sides of brisket. Season both sides with garlic salt and pepper. Place brisket in smoker on meat grates. Cook at 225° F to 250° F for about 3 hours. Layer ½ of the onion slices and ½ of the jalapeños on large piece of heavy-duty foil. Place brisket on top of prepared layers. Top with remaining onion slices and jalapeños; seal tightly to prevent leakage. Place brisket in smoker. Cook for 3 hours longer. Remove brisket; discard foil. Slice and serve. Decrease amount of jalapeños for less heat.

Joe Davidson, Oklahoma Joe's

Oklahoma Joe Davidson is the 1995 inductee into the KCBS Hall of Fame. His award-winning cookers are used by some of the best competitors on the circuit.

SMOKED BARBEQUED BRISKET

Yield: 30 servings

½ cup barbeque spices	¼ cup Worcestershire sauce
½ cup red wine	1 tablespoon lemon juice
¼ cup soy sauce	1 (7- to 10-pound) beef
¼ cup packed brown sugar	brisket
¼ cup vegetable oil	

Pour mixture of barbeque spices, red wine, soy sauce, brown sugar, oil, Worcestershire sauce and lemon juice over brisket in large nonreactive dish, turning to coat. Marinate in refrigerator for 6 hours or longer, turning occasionally. Drain, reserving marinade. Place brisket in smoker. Cook at 200° F to 250° F for 10 to 12 hours or until cooked through, mopping with reserved marinade occasionally.

Bob Brown, Holy Smokers

The Holy Smokers team is comprised of church members. They have competed on the circuit for more than ten years.

'Que Tip

Buy short, thick, or whole briskets with a heavy layer of fat. The bigger the brisket the better for smoking.

TRI-TIP ROAST

Yield: 12 servings

½ cup olive oil	1 teaspoon thyme
½ cup balsamic vinegar	½ teaspoon cayenne
¼ cup orange juice	1 (3-pound) tri-tip beef roast
2 tablespoons lemon juice	
1 tablespoon onion powder	4 cloves of garlic, cut into slivers
1 tablespoon garlic powder	
1 tablespoon dry mustard	2 tablespoons vegetable oil
1 teaspoon rosemary	

Combine olive oil, balsamic vinegar, orange juice, lemon juice, onion powder, garlic powder, dry mustard, rosemary, thyme and cayenne in jar with tightfitting lid; shake to mix. Let stand at room temperature for several hours before using. Pierce roast 10 or more times with sharp knife; insert 1 garlic sliver into each slit. Brush with vegetable oil. Place roast in roasting rack in center of grill. Cook with lid down over indirect heat for 50 minutes for medium-rare, basting frequently with olive oil mixture. The tri-tip roast is one of the muscles of the sirloin. Ask your butcher for this cut.

Steve Tyler, **On The Grill: The Backyard Bungler's Barbecue Cookbook**

Steve Tyler, construction consultant turned cookbook writer, is author of
On The Grill: The Backyard Bungler's Barbecue Cookbook.

'Que Tip

If a fire is too hot, shut the dampers, mist with
water, raise the cooking grill, and close the cover or lid
to reduce the amount of oxygen available.

SHRIMP-STUFFED BEEF ROAST

Yield: 15 servings

½	cup chopped celery	¼	cup dry white wine
¼	cup chopped chives	¾	teaspoon lemon zest
2	tablespoons butter	⅛	teaspoon salt
12	ounces shrimp, cooked, peeled, chopped	⅛	teaspoon cracked pepper
½	cup plain croutons	1	(5-pound) boneless beef rib roast

Sauté celery and chives in butter in skillet until tender. Stir in shrimp, croutons, white wine, lemon zest, salt and pepper; mix well. Spread evenly over roast. Roll roast to enclose stuffing; secure with kitchen twine. Insert meat thermometer near center of roast. Arrange hot coals around drip pan in covered grill. Place roast on grill rack over drip pan, not coals. Cook with lid down for 2½ hours or to 140° F on meat thermometer for rare, for 3 hours or to 160° F on meat thermometer for medium or for 3½ hours or to 170 ° F on meat thermometer for well done. Let stand for 15 minutes before slicing.

Brenda Tunstill, Tunstill's Hot Off The Grill

Brenda Tunstill, of Tunstill's Hot Off The Grill in Ozark, Missouri, has won numerous ribbons at the Missouri State Fair and the Ozark Empire Fair.

'Que Tip

Cooking may be done with direct or indirect heat. Direct heat is obtained by distributing the coals evenly over the bottom of the grill. Indirect heat is obtained by moving the coals to one side and placing a foil drip pan under the meat in the middle area between the coals. Indirect heat cooks slower and is best for thick or large pieces of meat.

CHATEAUBRIAND EN PATE

Yield: 12 servings

16	ounces chicken livers	1	teaspoon pepper
½	medium onion, chopped	1	(3-pound) beef tenderloin
¼	cup butter	8	ounces bacon slices
2	hard-cooked eggs		

Rinse chicken livers; pat dry. Sauté livers and onion in butter in skillet until livers are cooked through and onion is tender. Process livers, onion, eggs and pepper in food processor until smooth. Let stand until cool. Grill tenderloin over hot coals until seared on all sides. Cool slightly. Spread pâté over tenderloin; wrap with bacon slices. Cook over indirect heat to 145° F on meat thermometer.

Rich & Bunny Tuttle, K-Cass Bar-B-Que

Rich and Bunny Tuttle and the four junior Tuttles are a true barbequing family. They camp out, compete, and truly enjoy each other.

GRILLED BEEF TENDERLOIN

Yield: 16 servings

½	cup olive oil	2	tablespoons liquid smoke
6	cloves of garlic, crushed	1	(4-pound) whole beef
½	cup teriyaki marinade		tenderloin, trimmed

Combine oil, garlic, teriyaki marinade and liquid smoke in sealable plastic bag; mix well. Add tenderloin. Squeeze air from bag, allowing marinade to cover tenderloin; seal. Marinate in refrigerator for 6 to 8 hours, turning occasionally; drain. Place tenderloin on grill rack over medium-hot coals. Grill with lid down for 12 minutes. Turn tenderloin over. Cook for 12 minutes longer or until done to taste. Cut into ½- to ¾-inch slices. Serve immediately.

Bill Simon, Three Alarm Smokers

GARLIC-STUDDED KANSAS CITY STRIP LOIN

Yield: 40 servings

1	(10- to 12-pound) beef strip loin	¼	cup seasoned salt
1	large head of garlic, separated into cloves, crushed	¼	cup coarsely ground pepper

Trim silver skin from bottom of strip loin; trim fat cap to ¼ inch. Make slits with sharp knife in strip loin; insert garlic cloves into slits. Sprinkle with seasoned salt and pepper. Place fat side up on grill rack in grill with water pan. Cook with lid down over medium heat for 2 hours. Turn strip loin over. Cook for 1 hour; turn. Cook for 30 minutes longer or to 140° F on meat thermometer for medium-rare.

Paul Kirk, K.C. Baron of Barbecue

Paul Kirk, K.C. Baron of Barbecue of Roeland Park, Kansas, has earned more that 375 ribbons and trophies in competition.

STUFFED LONDON BROIL

Yield: 4 servings

1	(2-pound) London broil or sirloin steak, 1½ inches thick	¼	cup chopped fresh chives or green onions
¼	cup chopped sun-dried tomatoes marinated in olive oil	2	cloves of garlic, minced
		½	teaspoon pepper
		1	tablespoon Worcestershire sauce

Cut a horizontal pocket halfway through the London broil. Spoon mixture of sun-dried tomatoes, chives, garlic and pepper into pocket; close pocket. Brush both sides of London broil with Worcestershire sauce. Cook over medium-hot coals for 12 minutes. Turn beef over. Cook for 8 minutes longer. Slice diagonally into ½-inch strips.

*Steve Tyler, **On The Grill: The Backyard Bungler's Barbecue Cookbook***

BARBEQUED FLANK STEAK

Yield: 4 servings

1	(1½-pound) flank steak	½	cup packed brown
½	cup vegetable oil		sugar
½	cup tomato juice	3	cloves of garlic, minced
½	cup soy sauce	½	teaspoon pepper

Score flank steak ⅛ inch deep on each side in diamond pattern, using sharp knife. Place in glass dish. Pour mixture of remaining ingredients over steak, turning to coat. Marinate, covered, in refrigerator for 24 hours, turning occasionally. Let stand at room temperature for 2 hours. Drain, reserving marinade. Bring reserved marinade to a boil in saucepan; strain into another saucepan. Keep warm over low heat. Grill steak over hot coals for 4 to 5 minutes per side or until done to taste. Slice steak cross grain into thin strips. Serve topped with warm marinade.

Paris Permenter & John Bigley, co-authors of **Texas Barbecue**

Paris Permenter & John Bigley traveled the state of Texas in search of the best barbeque. Their search was not in vain.

GRILLED PORTERHOUSE STEAKS

Yield: 8 servings

2	(2-pound) porterhouse steaks	2	tablespoons minced basil
¼	cup olive oil	1	tablespoon freshly ground pepper
4	cloves of garlic, crushed	1	tablespoon seasoned salt

Rub both sides of the steaks with mixture of olive oil, garlic and basil; sprinkle with pepper and seasoned salt. Grill steaks over medium-hot coals for 9 to 10 minutes per side for rare.

Paul Kirk, K.C. Baron of Barbecue

Paul Kirk, K.C. Baron of Barbecue, teaches hands-on barbeque instruction classes across the country. His former students are now beginning to beat him in barbeque competitions. He is happy for them . . . well, most of the time!

HAPPY "HOLLA" BRANDY PEPPER STEAK

Yield: 6 servings

1	(2-pound) sirloin steak, 1½ to 2 inches thick	1½	teaspoons salt
2	teaspoons coarsely ground pepper	½	cup Schlivovitz plum brandy
½	cup beef bouillon	1	teaspoon cornstarch
		2	tablespoons water

Trim fat from steak, reserving fat. Heat large skillet and render some of reserved fat. Sprinkle both sides of steak with pepper. Place steak in prepared skillet. Cook for 2 minutes on each side or until brown; reduce heat. Cook for 8 to 10 minutes or until steak is done to taste. Remove steak to warm platter. Drain pan drippings, reserving 2 teaspoons. Combine reserved pan drippings, bouillon, salt and brandy in same skillet. Cook until reduced by ¼, stirring constantly. Stir in mixture of cornstarch and water. Cook until thickened, stirring constantly. Pour over steak. Slice steak thinly cross grain. May add mushrooms to sauce. Schlivovitz plum brandy should be used when available.

Ed Roith, Happy "Holla" Bar-B-Q

Ed Roith, of the Happy "Holla" Bar-B-Q team of Shawnee, Kansas, has won seven state championship barbeque titles.

'Que Tip

Steaks should be cut one and one-half inches thick for grilling. Lean cuts may be wrapped in bacon to improve flavor and retain moistness.

MIXED FAJITAS ON THE GRILL

Yield: 24 servings

2	tablespoons salt	1½	pounds whole boneless skinless chicken breasts, cut into halves
2	(1½-pound) live lobsters		
2	cups tomato hot salsa	2¼	pounds skirt steak, cut into 2 or 3 pieces
1	cup chopped red onion		
1	cup packed fresh cilantro	18	large shrimp, peeled, deveined
4	jalapeños, chopped		
¼	cup gold tequila	24	(6-inch) flour tortillas, heated
¼	cup fresh lime juice		
1	teaspoon salt		
1	cup amber beer		

Bring enough water to cover lobsters and 2 tablespoons salt to a boil in stockpot. Add lobsters. Cook for 10 minutes, stirring once or twice; lobster tails, when straightened, should snap back in place and lobster meat should be almost fully cooked. Cool lobsters in colander. Crack claws and body shell; remove lobster meat in large pieces. Chill, covered, in refrigerator. Process salsa, onion, cilantro, jalapeños, tequila, lime juice and 1 teaspoon salt in food processor until puréed. Stir in beer. Rinse chicken; pat dry. Arrange chicken, skirt steak, shrimp and lobster in 2 or 3 shallow nonreactive dishes. Pour salsa mixture over top, turning to coat. Marinate, covered, in refrigerator for 2 hours, stirring once or twice. Drain, reserving marinade. Thread shrimp on skewers. Arrange skirt steak on grill rack 6 inches from heat source; spoon half the reserved marinade over the steaks. Grill with lid down over medium-high coals for 7 minutes. Turn steak over. Arrange chicken, lobster meat and shrimp skewers on grill rack. Baste with remaining marinade. Grill with lid down for 3½ minutes longer. Turn chicken, lobster meat and shrimp. Grill with lid down for 3½ minutes longer or until steaks are medium-rare and chicken, lobster meat and shrimp are light brown and cooked through. Transfer steaks and chicken to cutting board; tent with foil. Let stand for 10 minutes. Slice steak and chicken cross grain into ¼-inch strips. Arrange steak, chicken, lobster and shrimp on warm platter. Serve with warm tortillas. Garnish with pico de gallo and guacamole.

W. Park Kerr, **Texas Border Cookbook**

KANSAS CITY STRIP STEAKS

Yield: 4 servings

2	cups butter, softened	½	cup sugar
½	medium onion, minced	½	cup packed brown sugar
3	cloves of garlic, minced	½	cup paprika
2	tablespoons chopped fresh parsley	2	tablespoons salt
1	tablespoon chopped fresh thyme		Pepper to taste
			Cayenne to taste
4	(14-ounce) Kansas City strip steaks		Thyme and celery seeds to taste
	Worcestershire sauce to taste		

Combine butter, onion, garlic, parsley and 1 tablespoon thyme in bowl; mix well. Set aside. Pat steaks dry with paper towel. Drizzle both sides of steaks with Worcestershire sauce just until moistened. Pat mixture of sugar, brown sugar, paprika and salt on both sides of steaks; sprinkle both sides with pepper, cayenne, thyme to taste and celery seeds. Let steaks stand at room temperature for 1 hour. Grill steaks over hot coals until done to taste, turning once or twice. Serve with the butter mixture.

"Chef Dan" Morey, Team K.C.

Dan Morey, Certified Working Chef, is the originator of Chef Dan's barbeque sauces. He was a member of Team Kansas City, two-time winners of the World Championship Barbecue Contest in Lisdoonvarna, Ireland.

'Que Tip

Turn food with tongs or spatula to
prevent juices from escaping.

Beef

GRILLED KANSAS CITY STRIP STEAKS

Yield: 2 servings

2	cloves of garlic, minced	1	teaspoon paprika
¾	teaspoon salt	½	teaspoon pepper
1	tablespoon fresh lemon juice	¼	teaspoon low-sodium beef bouillon granules
2	teaspoons sugar	2	(8-ounce) Kansas City strip steaks, 1 inch thick
2	teaspoons prepared horseradish		

Combine garlic and salt in bowl, stirring until of the consistency of thick paste. Stir in lemon juice, sugar, horseradish, paprika, pepper and bouillon. Spread on both sides of steaks. Marinate, covered with plastic wrap, in refrigerator for 1 hour. Grill steaks over hot coals until done to taste.

Paul Kirk, K.C. Baron of Barbecue

Paul Kirk, K.C. Baron of Barbecue, has developed a line of sauces,
rubs, and salsas. These products have won many awards at the American
Royal International Barbecue Sauce Contest.

'Que Tip

Get to know your butcher. Do not be afraid to
ask him to trim a brisket or cut a steak a certain thickness.
Experiment with different cuts of meat to determine
which you and your family prefer. Refer to
Cutting Up in the Kitchen by Merle Ellis (available
through KCBS) to find out about varieties, cost-saving
meat buying, and usage.

RUTHERFORD'S BLACK JACK "DRUNK STEAK"

Yield: 4 servings

¼ (to ½) cup Jack Daniel's whiskey
4 (8-ounce) Kansas City strip steaks
1 cup beef broth

2 tablespoons soy sauce
1 tablespoon brown sugar
1 teaspoon cornstarch
2 tablespoons water

Pour just enough whiskey into shallow nonreactive dish to cover bottom. Add steaks, turning to coat. Marinate in refrigerator for 2 hours, turning frequently. Drain, reserving marinade. Bring reserved marinade, beef broth, soy sauce and brown sugar to a boil in saucepan, stirring frequently. Add mixture of cornstarch and water gradually, stirring until of the desired consistency. Set aside; keep warm. Grill steaks over hot coals until done to taste. Serve with warm whiskey sauce. For a thrill, pour 1 tablespoon heated whiskey over steaks and ignite. Serve steaks flaming.

Ralph Blevins, Rutherford's Ol' South

Ralph Blevins, of Rutherford's Ol' South in Sparks, Nevada, is a true barbeque entrepreneur. He is a restaurateur, caterer, franchisor, and has his own line of gourmet food products.

'Que Tip

To prevent steaks or chops from curling, slash edge of fat at two- to three-inch intervals. Cut fat to the edge of the meat.

EASY T-BONE STEAKS

Yield: 4 servings

1	(10-ounce) bottle (or less) Worcestershire sauce	¼	cup olive oil
		2	tablespoons garlic salt
4	(14-ounce) T-bone steaks	1	tablespoon ground pepper

Pour just enough Worcestershire sauce on both sides of steaks to moisten; coat with olive oil. Season with garlic salt and pepper. Grill steaks over medium-hot coals for 6 to 8 minutes per side for medium-rare or until done to taste.

Amy Winn

Amy Winn hates to cook! She developed this recipe that even she could not foul up. Quick, simple, and delicious.

BARBEQUED BEEF SHORT RIBS

Yield: 12 servings

4	cups water	2	tablespoons gingerroot, chopped
1½	cups soy sauce		
1	cup sugar	1	tablespoon honey
10	cloves of garlic, chopped	2	teaspoons hot pepper sauce
4	green onions, chopped		
3	tablespoons sesame seeds	5	(to 6) pounds beef short ribs
3	tablespoons sesame oil		

Mix first 10 ingredients in bowl. Add short ribs, turning to coat. Marinate, covered, in refrigerator for 24 hours, turning occasionally. Drain, reserving marinade. Grill with lid down over hot coals for 2 hours or until cooked through, turning and basting with reserved marinade 2 or more times.

Bob Lyon

Bob Lyon and his Beaver Castors Barbecue team of Bellevue, Washington, have qualified for every Jack Daniel's World Championship Barbecue Cooking Contest since its inception in 1989.

BORDER BURGERS

Yield: 8 servings

2	pounds lean ground beef	4	hamburger buns, separated
1	(4-ounce) can diced green chiles	2	(15-ounce) cans chili with beans, heated
¾	cup finely shredded Cheddar cheese	¾	cup finely shredded Cheddar cheese
½	teaspoon salt	1	cup chopped red onion
½	teaspoon pepper		
½	teaspoon cumin		

Combine ground beef, green chiles, ¾ cup Cheddar cheese, salt, pepper and cumin in bowl; mix well. Shape into eight ¾-inch thick patties. Grill 4 to 6 inches above hot coals for 8 minutes for rare, 12 minutes for medium and 15 minutes for well-done, turning once or twice. Move patties to edge of grill. Place buns cut side down on grill. Grill for 1 minute or until light brown. Remove from grill. Arrange patties on buns on serving platter. Top with chili; sprinkle with ¾ cup cheese and onion.

Donna McClure, PDT (Pretty Damn Tasty)

---

*Donna McClure is an avid volunteer in her home town of Lenexa, Kansas. She chaired the Lenexa Historical Society cookbook, **Spinach Tyme**. Lenexa was dubbed the "Spinach Capital of the World" in the 1930s.*

'Que Tip

A marinade usually tenderizes approximately one-fourth inch beneath the surface of the meat.

SMOKED MEAT LOAF

Yield: 24 servings

4	pounds ground beef	3	tablespoons Italian
2	pounds ground pork		seasoning
1	cup dry bread crumbs	¾	cup barbeque sauce
1	egg, beaten	1	cup (or more) apple juice
	Salt and pepper to taste		

Combine ground beef, ground pork, bread crumbs, egg, salt, pepper, Italian seasoning and barbecue sauce in bowl; mix well. Shape into 2-inch thick oval. Place in smoker on heavy-duty foil. Smoke with apple wood chips over low heat for 6 hours or until cooked through, basting with apple juice occasionally. Let stand for 30 minutes before slicing.

Kathy LaBelle, Big Art's Dino Cookers

WARM-YOU-UP CHILI

Yield: 6 servings

1	pound chopped beef	3	tablespoons chili powder
½	cup chopped onion	1	tablespoon molasses
1	(16-ounce) can red beans	1	teaspoon chopped hot red
1	(16-ounce) can refried		pepper
	beans	½	teaspoon salt
1	(8-ounce) can tomato	½	teaspoon garlic salt
	sauce	⅛	teaspoon pepper
1	cup water	⅛	teaspoon cayenne

Brown chopped beef with onion in heavy saucepan; drain. Add red beans, refried beans, tomato sauce, water, chili powder, molasses, red pepper, salt, garlic salt, pepper and cayenne; mix well. Simmer, covered, for 3 to 4 hours or until of the desired consistency, stirring occasionally.

Hoelting Brothers

SAUSAGE

~❧~

MASTER STEPS FOR MAKING SAUSAGE

You use many of these same steps when making: (1) standard bulk sausage, (2) sausages with a casing, and (3) sausages without a casing. Prepare sausage meats according to a *Barbecuing & Sausage-Making Secrets* recipe or use your own recipe. Each kind of sausage uses (1) a distinct spice/seasoning recipe and (2) a meat recipe.

Step 1: Select a spice/seasoning mixture for your sausage.

Step 2: Meat preparation: Trim excess fat, if desired. Cut meat into pieces that will go through the throat of your grinder or food processor. If using frozen ground meat, thaw first.

Step 3: Coarsely grind meat over the sausage plate, 3/16-inch diameter holes or larger.

Step 4: Mix the recipe's liquid/spice seasoning mixture. The liquid may be water, milk, beer, wine, or brandy.

Step 5: Mix ground meat with the liquid mixture. Fine grind over the hamburger plate, 1/8-inch diameter holes. This is not necessary for finely pre-ground meat such as frozen ground chicken or turkey. Package sausage for the refrigerator or freezer if you don't stuff it or make sausage without casings.

Charlie & Ruthie Knote, **Barbecuing & Sausage-Making Secrets**

BOCKWURST

Yield: 40 servings

5	pounds Boston butt or pork shoulder, cut up	4	teaspoons non-iodized salt
1	bunch parsley	1	tablespoon plus 2 teaspoons nutmeg
3	large green onions with tops	2	teaspoons white pepper
1/2	small onion	1 1/2	teaspoons sugar
2	eggs	1	teaspoon MSG
3/4	cup milk	2	teaspoons thyme

Force pork through meat grinder fitted with sausage plate, $3/16$-inch diameter holes, into bowl. Force parsley, green onions and onion through meat grinder into bowl; press a small amount of ground pork through grinder to push any remaining particles of ground vegetables into bowl. Whisk eggs and milk in bowl until blended. Add parsley mixture, salt, nutmeg, white pepper, sugar, MSG and thyme; mix well. Add to pork; mix well. Force pork mixture through meat grinder fitted with hamburger plate, $1/8$-inch diameter holes. Stuff into casings 31 to 34 millimeters in diameter and link. Cook as desired.

Charlie & Ruthie Knote, **Barbecuing & Sausage-Making Secrets**

Charlie and Ruthie Knote offer a barbeque correspondence course. This intensive self-study program will educate both the novice and the intermediate outdoor chef.

'Que Tip

If not available in the meat case at your local supermarket, ask the butcher for lean ground pork made from pork shoulder butt or picnic roasts for making sausage.

CHORIZO SAUSAGE

Yield: 40 servings

5	pounds ground pork shoulder or butt	1	teaspoon coriander
12	ounces pork fat	1	teaspoon cumin
5	cloves of garlic, crushed	1	teaspoon black pepper
2	tablespoons paprika	1	teaspoon cinnamon
1	tablespoon oregano	1⅓	cups water
5	teaspoons salt	⅔	cup white vinegar
4	teaspoons crushed red pepper	¼	cup water

Combine ground pork and pork fat in bowl; mix well. Combine garlic, paprika, oregano, salt, red pepper, coriander, cumin, black pepper and cinnamon in bowl; mix well. Stir in 1⅓ cups water and vinegar. Add vinegar mixture to pork ¼ at a time, mixing well after each addition. Stuff into pork or beef casings. Place links in cold skillet. Add ¼ cup water. Simmer, covered, for 5 minutes; drain. Cook, uncovered, over low heat for 12 to 15 minutes or until cooked through, turning occasionally. Grill over direct or indirect heat until cooked through.

Paul Kirk, K.C. Baron of Barbecue

'Que Tip

On March 5, 1985, $56,000 was paid for a crossbreed barrow named "Bud," owned by Jeffrey Roemisch of Hermleigh, Texas, and bought by E. A. "Bud" Olson and Phil Bonzio. This is the highest known price ever paid for a hog.

CREOLE PORK SAUSAGE

Yield: 40 servings

2 tablespoons granulated onion	1 teaspoon crushed red pepper
2 tablespoons seasoned salt	½ teaspoon cayenne
2 tablespoons parsley flakes	½ teaspoon allspice
1 tablespoon paprika	¼ teaspoon ground bay leaf
1 tablespoon granulated garlic	½ cup water
1 tablespoon black pepper	5 pounds (sausage grind) ground pork shoulder

Mix onion, seasoned salt, parsley flakes, paprika, garlic, black pepper, red pepper, cayenne, allspice and bay leaf in bowl. Stir in water. Add gradually to pork in bowl, mixing well after each addition. Stuff into 5 yards of sausage casings. Smoke or barbeque on grill.

Beverly Norris, Possum Town Pork Forkers

HOT ITALIAN PEPPER SAUSAGE

Yield: 40 servings

2 tablespoons seasoned salt	1 tablespoon paprika
2 tablespoons crushed red pepper	2 teaspoons fennel seeds
1 tablespoon granulated onion	¼ teaspoon ground bay leaf
1 tablespoon granulated garlic	¼ teaspoon thyme
1 tablespoon black pepper	¼ teaspoon coriander
	½ cup cold water
	5 pounds coarsely ground pork shoulder

Combine seasoned salt, red pepper, onion, garlic, black pepper, paprika, fennel seeds, bay leaf, thyme and coriander in bowl; mix well. Stir in cold water. Add spice mixture to pork in bowl gradually, mixing well after each addition. Stuff into 2½ yards of sausage casings. Smoke, grill or barbeque. Decrease red pepper to 1 tablespoon for milder flavor.

Beckie Baker, Powderpuff Barbeque

HOT LINKS
Yield: 80 servings

5   tablespoons Morton Tender-Quick

3   tablespoons onion powder

3   tablespoons paprika

2   tablespoons garlic powder

2   tablespoons black pepper

2   tablespoons chopped chives

1   tablespoon crushed red pepper

2½ teaspoons cayenne

2   cups ice water

10 pounds boned pork butt, coarsely ground

Combine Tender-Quick, onion powder, paprika, garlic powder, black pepper, chives, red pepper and cayenne in large bowl; mix well. Stir in ice water. Add pork; mix well. Stuff into 32- to 35-millimeter diameter casings, making links about 6 inches long. Hang on rack or place on grill. Smoke in smoker at 110° F to 130° F for 3 to 6 hours. Increase temperature to 160° F. Cook until internal temperature reaches 155° F on meat thermometer. Remove sausage; spray with water to cool. Store in refrigerator or freezer. May add 3 tablespoons MSG to pork mixture.

Mike Taege, Mr. T

'Que Tip
A single sausage measuring 5,917 feet in length was cooked in Barcelona, Spain, on September 22, 1986.

HAPPY "HOLLA" KIELBASA

Yield: 24 servings

2 pounds pork butt with some fat, medium grind	1 tablespoon kosher salt
1 pound beef chuck, medium ground	1 teaspoon marjoram
3 tablespoons minced garlic	1 teaspoon coriander
2 tablespoons coarsely ground pepper	1 teaspoon dry mustard
1 tablespoon sugar	¾ teaspoon cayenne
	½ teaspoon freshly grated nutmeg
	1 cup water

Combine pork and beef in bowl; mix well. Combine minced garlic, pepper, sugar, kosher salt, marjoram, coriander, dry mustard, cayenne and nutmeg in bowl; mix well. Add spice mixture and water to pork mixture, kneading until blended. Chill, covered, for 12 hours; mix. Stuff into casings or shape into rolls of desired size and wrap with heat-resistant plastic wrap. A water smoker is best for this sausage, but any type of smoker will give good results. Ideal smoking temperatures are between 170° F and 250° F. If using plastic wrap, place in smoker at 250° F for about 30 minutes. This will allow sausage to become firm. Remove plastic wrap; reduce smoker temperature. Smoke until meat thermometer inserted 2 to 3 inches into end of sausage registers 160° F. Follow same directions for links, disregarding instructions for plastic wrap.

Ed Roith, Happy "Holla" Bar-B-Q

'Que Tip

Today's average pork loin cuts average fewer
than 165 calories per three-ounce serving.

POLISH KIELBASA

Yield: 40 servings

1	tablespoon garlic powder	½	teaspoon MSG
1	tablespoon salt	1	cup water
4	teaspoons pepper	3½	pounds coarsely ground
4	teaspoons marjoram		pork butt, pork shoulder
2½	teaspoons Morton		or picnic
	Tender-Quick	1½	pounds lean beef,
1¼	teaspoons allspice		coarsely ground
1	teaspoon sugar		

Combine garlic powder, salt, pepper, marjoram, Tender-Quick, allspice, sugar and MSG in bowl; mix well. Stir in water. Add pork and beef; mix well. Press pork mixture through food grinder fitted with hamburger plate, ⅛-inch diameter holes, into bowl. Stuff into casings and link. Wood smoke until sausage has a good brown color and reaches a temperature of 155° F.

Charlie & Ruthie Knote, **Barbecuing & Sausage-Making Secrets**

Charlie is known for attending cook-offs to promote his book.
Frequently, he will bring one of his excellent homemade sausages, and Ruthie
will offer her great Friendship Bread.

'Que Tip

If using charcoal to grill, it will take thirty to
forty-five minutes before the coals are ready. Do not
start grilling before the coals are covered with a light
ash. The coals should not be flaming.

MR. T'S ITALIAN SAUSAGE

Yield: 80 servings

6	tablespoons salt	1	tablespoon crushed red
2	tablespoons Italian seasoning		pepper
1	tablespoon cracked fennel seeds	2	cups ice water
1	tablespoon sugar	10	pounds boneless pork butt, ground

Combine salt, Italian seasoning, fennel seeds, sugar and red pepper in bowl; mix well. Stir in ice water. Combine spice mixture with pork in bowl; mix well. Stuff into 20 feet of 32- to 35-millimeter casings, making links about 6 inches long; form into ring. Cook as desired.

Mike Taege, Mr. T

GRILLED LAMB SAUSAGE

Yield: 16 servings

1	pound boneless lamb shoulder	1	tablespoon cold water
1	pound pork butt	5	teaspoons salt
4	ounces fresh fatback	1	teaspoon sugar
2	cloves of garlic, crushed	³/₄	teaspoon cumin
3	tablespoons chopped fresh cilantro		Freshly ground pepper to taste

Cut lamb, pork and fatback into 2-inch cubes. Chill, covered, in refrigerator. Force lamb, pork and fatback through food grinder fitted with medium-to-large plate into bowl. Add garlic, cilantro, cold water, salt, sugar, cumin and ground pepper; mix well. Stuff into casings. Cook as desired.

Paul Kirk, K.C. Baron of Barbecue

PISTACHIO SAUSAGE

Yield: 24 servings

3 pounds coarsely ground pork butt	1 teaspoon coarsely ground black pepper
½ cup whole shelled pistachios	½ teaspoon crushed red pepper
1 clove of garlic, minced	Coarsely ground black pepper to taste
1 tablespoon salt	
1 tablespoon chopped fresh parsley	

Combine pork, pistachios, garlic, salt, parsley, 1 teaspoon black pepper and red pepper in bowl; mix well. Divide into 4 portions. Shape each portion into roll 1½ inches in diameter; wrap in plastic wrap. Store in refrigerator until just before cooking. Discard plastic wrap. Coat surface of sausage with black pepper to taste. Grill over hot coals until cooked through and brown, turning frequently.

Janeyce Michel-Cupito, Powderpuff Barbeque

'Que Tip

During the War of 1812, a New York pork packer named Uncle Sam Wilson shipped a boatload of several hundred pounds of pork to U.S. troops. Each barrel was stamped "U.S." On the docks, it quickly became bantered about that the "U.S." stood for "Uncle Sam," whose large pork shipment looked to be large enough to feed the entire army. Thus, it is said, "Uncle Sam" came to represent the U.S. Government.

SEAFOOD SAUSAGE

Yield: 20 servings

2	teaspoons unflavored gelatin	¼	cup chopped onion
¼	cup cold water	¼	cup chopped pimento-stuffed olives
½	cup boiling water	2	tablespoons lemon juice
2	cups chopped uncooked mixed seafood	2	tablespoons chopped fresh dillweed
1½	cups mayonnaise	1½	teaspoons paprika
1	cup finely chopped celery	½	teaspoon Tabasco sauce
1	cup finely chopped carrot		

Soften gelatin in cold water; mix well. Add to boiling water in bowl, stirring until gelatin dissolves. Stir in seafood, mayonnaise, celery, carrot, onion, olives, lemon juice, dillweed, paprika and Tabasco sauce. Stuff into small sausage casings. Chill until firm. Arrange sausages on heavy-duty foil on grill rack. Grill over medium-hot coals for 15 to 20 minutes or until cooked through, turning every 5 minutes. Use alder or fruitwoods if smoking. May spoon sausage mixture into mold, chill until firm and grill over hot coals.

Hal Walker, Hasty-Bake Ole Smokers

In "real life" Hal Walker is a lawyer for the city of Kansas City, Kansas. He has won several awards in the "Anything Butt" competition at Memphis in May.

'Que Tip

Fresh fish, or properly frozen and thawed fish,
has little odor. Use your nose as a guide to freshness.

LAMB

∽∾

BARBEQUED LEG OF LAMB

Yield: 12 servings

1	(4-pound) leg of lamb, boned, rolled, tied	1	tablespoon coarsely ground pepper
¼	cup olive oil	1	teaspoon basil
2	tablespoons garlic salt		

Rub lamb with olive oil; sprinkle with garlic salt, pepper and basil. Cook in smoker at 250° F over indirect heat for 4 hours or to 140° F on meat thermometer for medium-rare. Serve with your favorite barbeque sauce or mint sauce.

Paul Kirk, K.C. Baron of Barbecue

Paul Kirk, K.C. Baron of Barbecue, has more than one thousand volumes in his cookbook collection.

BBQ LEG OF LAMB
Yield: 12 servings

1	cup mayonnaise	¼	cup Hungarian paprika
¼	cup lemon juice	½	cup packed brown sugar
3	tablespoons prepared horseradish	1	(4-pound) leg of lamb, butterflied, trimmed
1	tablespoon Worcestershire sauce	10	large cloves of garlic, minced
2	tablespoons grated onion	½	teaspoon salt
1	tablespoon tomato paste	½	cup olive oil
4	cups cider vinegar	1	bunch parsley, minced

Combine mayonnaise, lemon juice, horseradish, Worcestershire sauce, onion and tomato paste in bowl; mix well. Chill, covered, in refrigerator; flavor is enhanced if prepared 3 to 4 days in advance. Combine vinegar, paprika and brown sugar in saucepan; mix well. Cook until brown sugar dissolves, stirring frequently. Let stand until cool. Pour over lamb in shallow nonreactive dish, turning to coat. Marinate, covered, in refrigerator for 8 hours or longer, turning occasionally. Mash garlic and salt in bowl. Stir in olive oil and parsley. Store, covered, in refrigerator. Drain lamb, discarding marinade. Pat lamb dry with paper towel. Sear both sides of lamb over hot coals. Cook over indirect heat for 45 to 60 minutes or until done to taste, basting with garlic mixture until completely used. Remove lamb from grill; wrap in foil. Let stand for 15 minutes. Slice across grain. Arrange on serving platter. Serve with chilled horseradish sauce.

David Veljacic

David Veljacic and his wife, Pat, have a barbeque team called Sum Young Guy. They are the organizers of the British Columbia Championship in Vancouver, British Columbia.

BARBEQUED LEG OF LAMB A LA DEE'S DINER

Yield: 15 servings

1	(5-pound) leg of lamb, butterflied	1	cup chopped garlic
1	cup red wine	4	bay leaves
1	cup soy sauce	1	tablespoon crushed red chile
1	cup olive oil		

Pierce lamb on all sides with fork or ice pick. Place in sealable plastic bag. Pour mixture of remaining ingredients over lamb. Remove air from bag; seal. Marinate in refrigerator for 2 days, turning occasionally. Drain, reserving marinade. Place lamb on grill rack with drip pan underneath. Grill at 225° F to 275° F over indirect heat for 3 hours or until done to taste, basting with reserved marinade every 20 minutes. Serve with rosemary- and garlic-roasted potatoes.

Deanna Desin

CHINESE-STYLE LAMB

Yield: 20 servings

¼	cup soy sauce	1	piece of gingerroot, peeled, sliced, or ½ teaspoon ground ginger
¼	cup lemon juice		
¼	cup honey		
1	clove of garlic, minced	1	(4- to 7-pound) leg of lamb, butterflied
1	teaspoon pepper		

Process soy sauce, lemon juice, honey, garlic, pepper and gingerroot in food processor or blender until smooth. Pour over lamb in shallow nonreactive dish, turning to coat. Marinate, covered, in refrigerator for up to 12 hours, turning occasionally. Drain, reserving marinade. Grill 4 to 5 inches above hot coals for 35 to 45 minutes or until done to taste, turning and basting with reserved marinade occasionally.

Donna McClure, P.D.T. (Pretty Damn Tasty)

Donna McClure, P.D.T., is a former Grand Champion of the Great Pork BarbeQlossal, which is held in conjunction with the World Pork Expo in Des Moines, Iowa.

GOLDEN HEART LAMB

Yield: 12 servings

1	(3- to 4-pound) boned shoulder roast of lamb, rolled, tied	12	ounces dried apricots
	Salt and pepper to taste	1	(12-ounce) bottle creamy Italian salad dressing
		2	tablespoons minced garlic

Remove lamb from roasting net or untie twine. Trim off fat; sprinkle liberally with salt and pepper. Fold and tie lamb securely. Stuff interior of lamb with apricots. Place in sealable plastic bag. Pour mixture of salad dressing and garlic over lamb; seal bag. Marinate in refrigerator for 12 hours or longer. Drain, reserving marinade. Sear lamb over hot coals for 5 minutes on each side. Grill over low heat for $1^{1}/_{2}$ hours or until done to taste, basting with reserved marinade during first hour. Remove to serving platter; discard twine. Cut into thin slices.

Hal Walker, Hasty-Bake Ole Smokers

Hal Walker, of the Hasty-Bake Ole Smokers team of Kansas City, Kansas, has won several awards at the American Royal Barbecue Contest and The Great Lenexa Barbecue Battle with this recipe.

'Que Tip

Add a few sprigs of fresh rosemary to your gas or charcoal grill to impart a subtle suggestion of its flavor to lamb or vegetables.

HONEY-GRILLED SHOULDER OF LAMB

Yield: 12 servings

½ cup dry white wine	2 tablespoons lemon zest
½ cup finely minced onion	1 teaspoon salt
½ cup finely minced fresh mint or 1 tablespoon dried mint	¼ teaspoon pepper
	1 (3½- to 4-pound) shoulder of lamb, boned, rolled, tied
⅓ cup honey	
2 tablespoons lemon juice	

Pour mixture of first 8 ingredients over lamb in nonreactive dish, turning to coat. Marinate, covered, in refrigerator for 2 to 8 hours. Drain, reserving marinade. Grill lamb over hot coals to 140° F on meat thermometer for rare, 150° F on meat thermometer for medium or 160° F on meat thermometer for well-done, turning and brushing with reserved marinade occasionally. Remove lamb to serving platter; slice. Bring remaining marinade to a boil in saucepan. Serve with lamb.

Donna McClure, P.D.T. (Pretty Damn Tasty)

HAPPY "HOLLA" GRILLED LAMB CHOPS

Yield: 6 servings

6 lamb loin chops, 1 to 1½ inches thick, trimmed	1 teaspoon crushed rosemary
2 tablespoons olive oil	1 teaspoon thyme
2 tablespoons Dijon mustard	½ teaspoon pepper
2 tablespoons garlic powder	¼ teaspoon salt
	Salt and pepper to taste

Coat lamb chops with olive oil; spread Dijon mustard around edges of lamb chops. Roll the mustard-coated edges in mixture of garlic powder, rosemary, thyme, ½ teaspoon pepper and ¼ teaspoon salt. Sprinkle remaining surfaces with salt and pepper to taste. Grill lamb chops over hot coals to 144° F on meat thermometer.

Ed Roith, Happy "Holla" Bar-B-Q

LAMB CHOPS JALAPENO
Yield: 4 servings

1	(8-ounce) can juice-pack crushed pineapple	½	teaspoon salt
½	cup jalapeño jelly	4	lamb shoulder or rib chops, 1 inch thick
¼	cup fresh lemon juice	1	teaspoon salt
1	tablespoon prepared mustard	½	teaspoon pepper
		½	teaspoon cinnamon

Bring undrained pineapple, jelly, lemon juice, mustard and ½ teaspoon salt to a boil in saucepan. Boil until jelly melts, stirring constantly. Sprinkle both sides of lamb chops with mixture of 1 teaspoon salt, pepper and cinnamon. Grill lamb chops 4 inches above hot coals for 11 to 13 minutes per side or until done to taste. Spoon pineapple mixture over chops during last half of cooking process. May substitute apricot jam for pineapple mixture.

Donna McClure, P.D.T. (Pretty Damn Tasty)

'Que Tip

Do not start grilling until coals are at least eighty percent ashed over. If a fire is too cool, knock off some of the ashes and add charcoal around the edge.

SMOKED RACK OF LAMB
Yield: 6 servings

7 tablespoons club soda	1 whole rack of lamb, split, trimmed
3 tablespoons Jack Daniel's Black Label whiskey	1 cup currant jelly
⅓ cup barbeque spice	¾ cup chili sauce
1 teaspoon chopped fresh parsley	½ cup melted butter
⅛ teaspoon sage	3 tablespoons Jack Daniel's Black Label whiskey
⅛ teaspoon rosemary	1 tablespoon mint sauce
	Barbeque spice to taste

Pour mixture of club soda, 3 tablespoons whiskey, ⅓ cup barbeque spice, parsley, sage and rosemary over lamb in large nonreactive dish, turning to coat. Marinate, covered, in refrigerator for 8 hours or longer, turning occasionally. Combine currant jelly, chili sauce, butter, 3 tablespoons whiskey, mint sauce and barbeque spice to taste in bowl; mix well. Drain lamb, reserving marinade. Smoke lamb at 225° F over indirect heat for 1 hour. Remove lamb; slice into chops. Grill chops over direct heat until done to taste, turning and basting frequently with reserved marinade. Remove chops to serving platter; baste with some of the jelly mixture. Serve remaining jelly mixture with lamb chops.

Scott O'Meara, Yachtsman Bar-B-Q

'Que Tip
Sprinkle meat with seasonings at least one hour before cooking or, for enhanced flavor, marinate in refrigerator for eight hours or longer. Spray with nonstick cooking spray before and after applying seasonings.

MARINATED SMOKED LAMB STEAK

Yield: 2 servings

¼ cup chopped fresh rosemary

1 tablespoon minced fresh garlic

½ onion, chopped

2 cups virgin olive oil

1 (3-ounce) lamb steak (cut from leg), 3 inches thick

Process rosemary, garlic and onion in food processor fitted with steel blade until smooth. Add olive oil gradually, processing constantly until thickened. Pour over steak in nonreactive dish, turning to coat. Marinate, covered, in refrigerator for 4 to 8 hours, turning occasionally; drain. Grill steak over low heat to 140° F to 150° F on meat thermometer for rare, using cherry or apple wood chips. Fresh rosemary and garlic are a must in this recipe.

Curtis Shepard & Tim Lawrence

Curtis Shepard and Tim Lawrence of the Campbell Point Burnt Ends team are former Grand Champions of the American Royal Barbecue Contest.

BARBEQUED DENVER LAMB RIBS

Yield: 8 servings

8 (8-bone) slabs Denver lamb ribs, trimmed

2 tablespoons lemon pepper

1 tablespoon garlic salt

Sprinkle ribs with lemon pepper and garlic salt. Place ribs bone side down on grill rack. Grill over indirect heat for 45 minutes. Turn ribs. Grill for 30 minutes longer or until done to taste. Serve with mint or jalapeño jelly.

Ardie Davis

Ardie Davis, a.k.a. Remus Powers, Ph.B., is author of the official Barbeque Oath used to swear in judges at all KCBS-sanctioned contests.

HOT CHINESE LAMB RIBS

Yield: 8 servings

1	cup soy sauce	4	cloves of garlic, crushed
½	cup honey	2	teaspoons crushed red pepper
¼	cup packed light brown sugar	1	teaspoon red food coloring paste
¼	cup white vinegar	4	(1½-pound) slabs lamb spareribs, trimmed
¼	cup hoisin sauce		
2	tablespoons sherry		

Pour mixture of soy sauce, honey, brown sugar, vinegar, hoisin sauce, sherry, garlic, red pepper and food coloring over ribs in nonreactive dish, turning to coat. Marinate, covered, in refrigerator for 3 to 8 hours, turning occasionally. Drain, reserving marinade. Place ribs on grill rack bone side down. Grill with lid down over indirect heat for 45 minutes. Baste with reserved marinade; turn ribs. Grill for 30 minutes longer or until done to taste, basting with reserved marinade.

Paul Kirk, K.C. Baron of Barbecue

'Que Tip

Use branches of rosemary or fennel dipped in
vegetable oil to baste meats and vegetables.

LAMB KABOBS

Yield: 8 servings

½ cup lemon juice	1 large onion, cut into wedges
½ cup white wine	
2 tablespoons chopped onion	1 large green bell pepper, cut into chunks
2 tablespoons soy sauce	8 jalapeños, seeded, cut up
1½ tablespoons parsley flakes	2 large carrots, cut into chunks
1 teaspoon salt	
1 teaspoon pepper	2 medium potatoes, cut into chunks
2½ pounds lamb, cut into bite-size pieces	Garlic salt to taste

Pour mixture of lemon juice, white wine, 2 tablespoons onion, soy sauce, parsley flakes, salt and pepper over lamb in sealable plastic bag; seal bag. Marinate in refrigerator for 8 hours or longer, turning occasionally; drain. Thread lamb and vegetables alternately on skewers; sprinkle with garlic salt. Grill over hot coals until vegetables are tender and lamb is done to taste, turning occasionally.

Ernie Heimsoth, Chigger Creek

'Que Tip

For evenly cooked vegetables and meat kabobs, parboil
solid or starchy vegetables before they are threaded onto
skewers for grilling or smoking.

ROSEMARY-MARINATED LAMB KABOBS

Yield: 4 servings

½	cup orange juice	6	black peppercorns, crushed
¼	cup soy sauce		
¼	cup minced green onions	1	pound lamb, cut into 1-inch cubes
2	tablespoons teriyaki sauce		
2	tablespoons lime juice	3	green bell peppers, cut into 1-inch squares
2	tablespoons lemon juice		
2	tablespoons minced fresh rosemary, crushed	1	large onion, cut into 1-inch pieces
1	teaspoon chopped fresh garlic, crushed	2	large oranges, cut into 8 slices

Pour mixture of orange juice, soy sauce, green onions, teriyaki sauce, lime juice, lemon juice, rosemary, garlic and peppercorns over lamb in sealable plastic bag; seal bag. Marinate in refrigerator for 5 to 6 hours, turning occasionally; drain. Thread lamb alternately with green peppers and onion pieces onto skewers. Grill over hot coals for 8 to 10 minutes or until vegetables are tender and lamb is done to taste, turning frequently. Grill orange slices over hot coals just until heated through and marked, turning once. Arrange 2 orange slices on each plate; top with lamb kabobs.

Ardie Davis

'Que Tip

Skewer bay leaves with cubes of marinated lamb
or swordfish and roast over hot coals.

THAI LAMB KABOBS

Yield: 6 servings

1½ pounds lamb, cut into 1-inch cubes

1 (to 2) large Spanish onions, cut into 1-inch pieces

2 green bell peppers, cut into 1-inch squares

2 red bell peppers, cut into 1-inch squares

½ cup olive oil

⅓ cup unsweetened coconut milk

¼ cup lime juice

2 tablespoons minced fresh cilantro

2 teaspoons crushed red pepper

1 teaspoon cumin

1 teaspoon sea salt

1 clove of garlic, crushed

Thread lamb, onions, green peppers and red peppers alternately onto skewers. Place in large sealable plastic bags. Pour mixture of olive oil, coconut milk, lime juice, cilantro, red pepper, cumin, sea salt and garlic over lamb skewers; seal bags. Marinate in refrigerator for 4 to 6 hours, turning occasionally; drain. Grill lamb kabobs over medium-hot coals for 5 to 7 minutes per side for medium-rare or until done to taste. May substitute vegetable oil for olive oil.

John Baker, Powderpuff Barbeque

'Que Tip

Freeze onions for forty-five minutes before slicing or chopping. This will keep away the tears.

LAMB BURGERS WITH BERRY SAUCE
Yield: 6 servings

1¼	cups fresh mint leaves, finely chopped	3	green onions, thinly sliced
7	tablespoons raspberry vinegar	2	cloves of garlic, minced
1	tablespoon fresh lemon juice	8	ounces mild goat cheese, cut into 6 portions
3	tablespoons sugar	2	teaspoons garlic powder
	Salt and freshly ground pepper to taste	2	teaspoons onion powder
2	pounds ground lamb	1	teaspoon freshly ground pepper
3	tablespoons raspberry vinegar	1	teaspoon salt

Combine mint, 7 tablespoons raspberry vinegar, lemon juice, sugar and salt and pepper to taste in bowl, stirring until sugar dissolves. Set aside. Combine lamb, 3 tablespoons raspberry vinegar, green onions, garlic and salt and pepper to taste in bowl; mix well. Shape into 12 thin patties. Place 1 portion of goat cheese on half the patties. Top with remaining patties; seal edges. Sprinkle with mixture of garlic powder, onion powder, 1 teaspoon pepper and 1 teaspoon salt. Let stand at room temperature for 20 to 30 minutes. Cook in smoker at 200° F to 220° F for 40 minutes for medium-rare or to desired degree of doneness. Serve burgers hot with mint sauce. May baste burgers 1 or 2 times during cooking process with heated mixture of ½ cup raspberry vinegar and 2 tablespoons extra-virgin olive oil.

Cheryl Alters Jamison & Bill Jamison, **Smoke & Spice**

'Que Tip

Smoking should be done at 200° F to 220° F; if temperature gets too high, partially close the dampers, or if temperature is too low open the dampers and add additional wood.

SEAFOOD

~~

MESQUITE GRILLED AMBERJACK

Yield: 4 servings

Mesquite wood chips

2 large ripe avocados, cut into ½-inch cubes

1 cup fresh or frozen corn

¼ cup chopped onion

2 cloves of garlic, minced

1 tablespoon chopped cilantro

¼ teaspoon red pepper flakes

Juice of 1 lime

Salt to taste

4 (6- to 8-ounce) amberjack fillets

1 (to 2) tablespoons olive oil

Freshly ground red, green and black peppercorns to taste

Soak handful of mesquite wood chips in water in container. Combine avocados, corn, onion, garlic, cilantro, red pepper flakes, lime juice and salt in bowl, stirring gently. Let stand at room temperature for 1 hour before serving. Brush fillets lightly with olive oil; sprinkle with ground pepper and salt. Drain wood chips; sprinkle over hot coals. Grill fillets over hot coals for 5 minutes per side. Arrange fillets on serving platter. Serve with avocado corn salsa. Grill in covered grill for smokier flavor.

*Karen Adler, author of **Hooked on Fish on the Grill***

Karen is President of Pig Out Publications, which specializes in publishing and distributing barbeque and grill books.

LEMON GRILLED CATFISH

Yield: 6 servings

½	cup unsalted butter, softened	6	(5- to 7-ounce) catfish fillets
1	clove of garlic, crushed	2	tablespoons lemon pepper

Combine butter and garlic in bowl; mix well. Coat both sides of fillets lightly with some of the butter mixture; sprinkle with lemon pepper. Place fillets on grill rack in covered grill. Grill over medium-hot coals for 6 to 7 minutes. Turn and baste with remaining butter mixture. Grill for 5 minutes longer or until fish flakes easily. Serve with barbeque salsa or fruit salsa.

Carolyn Wells

STATE CHAMPIONSHIP SMOKED CATFISH

Yield: 6 servings

1	(2- to 3-pound) whole catfish, cleaned	¼	cup olive oil Salt to taste

Coat catfish with olive oil; sprinkle with salt. Coat large piece of cheesecloth liberally with additional oil; tie knot in end of cheesecloth. Place catfish head first in cheesecloth; hang with tail end up in smoker. Cook for 3 to 4 hours or until fish flakes easily. May grill over indirect heat if catfish cannot be hung in smoker.

Jessica Kirk

Jessica Kirk is a former Grand Champion of the Great Lenexa Barbecue Battle—the Kansas State Championship.

'Que Tip

Store fresh fish in its original wrapper in the coldest part of the refrigerator. Cook fresh fish within one to two days after purchasing.

MONKFISH WITH JALAPENOS & CILANTRO

Yield: 4 servings

1 cup chili sauce	¼ teaspoon freshly ground pepper
3 tablespoons minced fresh cilantro	1 (1½-pound) monkfish fillet, cut into 1x1½-inch cubes
1 tablespoon cider vinegar	
3 green onions with tops, minced	1 medium zucchini, cut into 35 (⅛-inch) slices
1½ teaspoons minced seeded fresh jalapeños	8 mushrooms
1½ teaspoons liquid smoke	1 red onion, cut into quarters, separated
¼ teaspoon chili powder	

Combine chili sauce, cilantro, cider vinegar, green onions, jalapeños, liquid smoke, chili powder and pepper in bowl; mix well. Let stand at room temperature for 4 hours to blend flavors. Pour over monkfish in nonreactive dish, turning to coat. Marinate, covered, in refrigerator for 8 hours or longer, stirring occasionally. Add zucchini, mushrooms and red onion to monkfish mixture 2 hours before skewering; mix well. Drain, discarding marinade. Thread monkfish, zucchini, mushrooms and onion alternately onto 8 skewers. Grill kabobs over medium-hot coals for 8 to 10 minutes, turning every 2 minutes. Remove to serving platter. Let stand, loosely covered, for 5 minutes before serving. Serve with home fries and red leaf lettuce salad with avocado. May assemble skewers 1 day in advance and refrigerate, covered, overnight. Let stand at room temperature for 20 minutes before grilling.

Leslie Beal Bloom, **Barbecue Sizzling Fireside Know-How**

'Que Tip

Rinse seafood in cold water to remove any
surface bacteria. Always marinate in the refrigerator,
not at room temperature.

GRILLED HALIBUT TARRAGON

Yield: 4 servings

½	cup melted butter	4	halibut steaks, 1 inch thick
¼	cup lemon juice		
4	teaspoons salt	4	teaspoons tarragon leaves

Combine butter, lemon juice and 2 teaspoons of the salt in bowl; mix well. Brush steaks with some of the butter mixture; rub mixture of remaining 2 teaspoons salt and tarragon on both sides of steaks. Place steaks in fish basket or on fish screen. Grill 5 inches above hot coals for 30 minutes or until fish flakes easily, turning once or twice and basting frequently with remaining butter mixture.

C.E. "Ol' Smokey" Tuttle, Chips Off Ol' Smokey

BBQ SALMON

Yield: 4 servings

8	large cloves of garlic, finely chopped	2	tablespoons minced sun-dried tomatoes
1	teaspoon salt	¼	cup olive oil
¼	cup finely chopped fresh parsley	1	(1½-pound) salmon fillet

Sprinkle garlic with salt in shallow dish; mash together with blade of knife. Combine with parsley, sun-dried tomatoes and olive oil in bowl; mix well. Let stand, covered, in refrigerator for 8 hours or longer. Cut 2 lengthwise slits to but not through skin with sharp knife. Spread half the garlic mixture over fillet and into slits. Place salmon skin side down on greased grill rack in covered grill. Grill with lid down over low heat for 10 to 15 minutes; spread with remaining garlic mixture. Cook with lid down over medium heat for 15 minutes or until fish flakes easily.

David Veljacic

David Veljacic, a Vancouver fireman, began barbequing competitively seven years ago. He has captured prizes internationally for his BBQ Salmon recipe and, in 1991, he was named the Canadian Barbecue Champion.

SMOKED SALMON WITH PEPPERCORN SAUCE

Yield: 2 servings

2	cups whipping cream	1	tablespoon brandy
¼	cup buttermilk, at room temperature	1	tablespoon port
1	(10-ounce) salmon steak, 1½ inches thick	1	teaspoon green peppercorns
¾	cup fish or chicken stock	10	pink peppercorns
			Salt to taste

Heat whipping cream in saucepan to 85° F. Remove from heat; stir in buttermilk. Let stand, covered, in warm place for 24 to 48 hours or until thickened. Store the crème fraîche in refrigerator until just before using. Cook salmon in smoker with cherry wood at 200° F for 3 to 4 hours or until salmon flakes easily. Boil stock, brandy, port and green peppercorns in saucepan until reduced to 2 tablespoons. Stir in 1¾ cups of the crème fraîche. Simmer until reduced to 1¼ cups, stirring occasionally. Stir in pink peppercorns and salt. Serve over salmon.

Tim Lawrence & Curtis Shepard, Campbell Point Burnt Ends

GRILLED SALMON STEAKS

Yield: 4 servings

6	tablespoons butter	2	tablespoons lemon juice
⅓	cup honey	1	teaspoon liquid smoke
⅓	cup packed dark brown sugar	⅛	teaspoon Tabasco sauce
		4	(8-ounce) salmon steaks

Combine butter, honey, brown sugar, lemon juice, liquid smoke and Tabasco sauce in saucepan. Cook over low heat for 5 minutes, stirring frequently. Let stand until cool. Pour over salmon in nonreactive dish, turning to coat. Let stand at room temperature for 30 minutes, turning once. Drain, reserving marinade. Grill steaks over hot coals for about 5 minutes per side, basting with reserved marinade. Allow 10 minutes total grilling time per inch of thickness of steaks.

Darrell & Karen DeGreve, Bearly Smokin'

SMOKED LAKE TROUT

Yield: 24 servings

1	gallon water	1	(8- to 12-pound) lake
½	cup salt		trout, cut into 3-inch
1	tablespoon pickling spice		pieces

Combine water and salt in large bowl, stirring until salt dissolves. Stir in pickling spice. Add trout pieces. Soak trout in salt solution in refrigerator or place on ice for 12 hours. Drain, discarding salt solution. Smoke trout in water smoker using oak wood chips at 170° F for 4 hours. May remove water pan 1 hour before end of smoking process for less moist fish.

Warren Fisher, Hi-Tech Smokers

---

*Warren Fisher of the Hi-Tech Smokers swears this recipe
works best on trout caught from Lake Superior.*

TROUT WITH LEMON ZEST BASTE

Yield: 2 servings

¼	cup butter	2	whole rainbow trout,
	Juice of 1 lemon		dressed
	Zest of 1 lemon		Salt and freshly ground
1	lemon, sliced		pepper to taste
½	small onion, sliced		

Heat butter in saucepan until melted. Stir in lemon juice and lemon zest. Set aside. Place 2 or 3 lemon slices and onion slices in cavity of each trout, reserving remaining lemon slices. Season with salt and pepper. Grill trout over hot coals for 6 to 7 minutes per side or until trout flakes easily, brushing with lemon butter mixture frequently. Remove to serving platter. Top with remaining lemon slices.

Karen Adler, author of **Hooked on Fish on the Grill**

SCALLOPS-ON-A-STICK

Yield: 4 servings

8	(10-inch) bamboo skewers	2	cloves of garlic, minced
2	tablespoons peanut oil	⅛	teaspoon hot sauce
2	tablespoons cream sherry	1½	pounds sea scallops
1	teaspoon dillweed	12	red medium-ripe cherry tomatoes
1	teaspoon onion powder	12	yellow pear tomatoes
½	teaspoon freshly ground white pepper		

Soak bamboo skewers in water for 20 minutes prior to use; drain. Combine peanut oil, sherry, dillweed, onion powder, white pepper, garlic and hot sauce in bowl; mix well. Add scallops and tomatoes, mixing to coat. Drain, discarding marinade. Thread scallops and tomatoes on skewers, alternating scallops and tomatoes of different colors. Grill kabobs over medium-hot coals for 3 minutes. Turn carefully, using spatula if necessary to assist turning. Grill for 2 to 3 minutes longer or until scallops are tender. Serve immediately.

Steve Tyler, **On The Grill: The Backyard Bungler's Barbecue Cookbook**

'Que Tip

Do not leave raw or cooked seafood out of the refrigerator for longer than two hours, including preparation time and time on the table.

BARBEQUED SHRIMP

Yield: 4 servings

1 cup butter	1 tablespoon pepper
¾ cup Worcestershire sauce	1 tablespoon salt
¾ cup lemon juice	1 teaspoon Louisiana hot
6 green onions, chopped	sauce
2 (to 4) cloves of garlic, minced	2½ pounds large shrimp, peeled, deveined

Heat butter in saucepan until melted. Stir in Worcestershire sauce, lemon juice, green onions, garlic, pepper, salt and Louisiana hot sauce. Let stand to blend flavors. Pour over shrimp in nonreactive dish, turning to coat. Marinate, covered, in refrigerator for desired amount of time, stirring occasionally. Drain, reserving marinade. Arrange shrimp on grill screen. Grill over hot coals until shrimp turn pink, turning and basting frequently with reserved marinade.

Donna McClure, P.D.T. (Pretty Damn Tasty)

GRILLED GINGER SHRIMP

Yield: 8 servings

1 cup minced green onions with tops	¼ cup grated gingerroot
½ cup salad oil	¼ cup lemon juice
½ cup soy sauce	1 tablespoon sugar
½ cup dry sherry	4 pounds (18- to 25-count) shrimp, peeled, deveined

Soak 16 bamboo skewers in water. Pour mixture of green onions, salad oil, soy sauce, sherry, gingerroot, lemon juice and sugar over shrimp in nonreactive dish, turning to coat. Marinate, covered, in refrigerator for 2 to 3 hours, stirring occasionally. Drain, discarding marinade. Thread shrimp on skewers. Grill over medium-hot coals for 3 minutes per side or until shrimp turn pink, turning once.

Jessica Kirk

HOT PEPPERED SHRIMP

Yield: 2 servings

2	scallions	1	teaspoon sugar
2	tablespoons peanut oil	1	clove of garlic, crushed
1	tablespoon catsup	½	teaspoon salt
1	tablespoon hot sauce	½	teaspoon cayenne
1	tablespoon soy sauce	1	pound shrimp, peeled,
2	teaspoons minced		deveined
	gingerroot		

Mince scallions, reserving green portion. Mix minced white portion of scallions with next 9 ingredients in nonreactive dish. Add shrimp, turning to coat. Marinate, covered, in refrigerator for 2 to 3 hours, stirring occasionally; drain. Thread shrimp on skewers. Grill over medium-hot coals for 5 to 7 minutes or until shrimp turn pink. Remove to serving platter. Sprinkle with reserved minced scallions.

Paul Kirk, K.C. Baron of Barbecue

MAC'S BBQ SHRIMP

Yield: 2 servings

12	jumbo shrimp, peeled, deveined	12	slices extra-thin peppered bacon
	Juice of 6 lemons		Cajun seasoning to taste

Combine shrimp and lemon juice in shallow nonreactive dish, turning to coat. Marinate, covered, in refrigerator for 8 hours, stirring occasionally. Drain, discarding lemon juice. Wrap each shrimp with 1 slice of bacon; secure with wooden pick. Sprinkle with Cajun seasoning. Grill over hot coals until bacon is crisp and shrimp turn pink, turning occasionally. May baste with your favorite barbeque sauce.

Mike McMillan, Mac's BBQ

Mike and Vickie McMillan own Mac's BBQ, a successful barbeque restaurant in Skiatook, Oklahoma. They are former Grand Champions of the Cherokee Strip Cook-Off in Ponca City, Oklahoma—The Oklahoma State Championship.

SPICY GOLDEN SHRIMP

Yield: 4 servings

2 cups plain yogurt	1 tablespoon Chinese hot mustard sauce
1 tablespoon black pepper	
1 tablespoon salt	1 teaspoon (scant) fennel seeds, crushed
1½ teaspoons crushed red pepper	
1 teaspoon saffron threads	1 teaspoon (scant) cumin
1 tablespoon lime juice	16 jumbo shrimp, peeled, deveined

Combine yogurt, black pepper, salt, red pepper and saffron threads in bowl; mix well. Chill, covered, for 24 hours. Add lime juice, hot mustard sauce, fennel seeds and cumin 3 to 4 hours before grilling; mix well. Fold in shrimp. Marinate, covered, in refrigerator for 2 hours or longer, stirring occasionally. Drain, reserving marinade. Thread shrimp onto skewers. Grill over medium-hot coals for 10 to 12 minutes or until shrimp turn pink, turning and basting frequently with reserved marinade.

Hal Walker, Hasty-Bake Ole Smokers

'Que Tip

Free-roaming hogs were notorious for rampaging through the grainfields of colonial New York City farmers. The Manhattan Island residents chose to limit the forays of these hogs by erecting a long, permanent wall on the northern edge of what is now Lower Manhattan. A street built to border this wall was named, aptly, Wall Street.

GAME

~~~

UNCLE BEAVER'S MARINATED DUCK BREASTS

Yield: 10 servings

5	whole duck breasts, split, boned	1	teaspoon Worcestershire sauce
2	cups zesty Italian salad dressing	1/2	teaspoon meat tenderizer
1/2	cup soy sauce	1/4	teaspoon garlic pepper
1/2	cup red wine	1/8	teaspoon tarragon
1	teaspoon garlic salt	1/8	teaspoon rosemary
1	teaspoon onion salt	10	thick slices bacon

Rinse duck and pat dry. Pour mixture of salad dressing, soy sauce, red wine, garlic salt, onion salt, Worcestershire sauce, meat tenderizer, garlic pepper, tarragon and rosemary over duck in nonreactive dish, turning to coat. Marinate, covered, in refrigerator for 8 hours or longer, turning frequently. Drain, reserving marinade. Wrap each duck breast with 1 slice of bacon; brush with reserved marinade. Grill as you would a small filet mignon.

Bubba Norris, Possum Town Pork Forkers

Bubba Norris, of the Possum Town Pork Forkers team of Columbus, Mississippi, is the organizer of the Possum Town Pig Fest—the Mississippi State Championship.

BARBEQUED ORANGE DUCK
Yield: 8 servings

2	(4- to 5-pound) ducks	2	oranges, cut into quarters
3	tablespoons olive oil	½	cup melted butter
1	tablespoon garlic salt	½	cup orange juice
2	teaspoons ground pepper	1	tablespoon minced parsley

Remove excess fat from ducks. Rinse and pat dry with paper towel. Rub ducks inside and outside with olive oil; sprinkle with garlic salt and pepper. Place 4 orange quarters inside each duck. Arrange ducks on grill rack in medium-hot grill with water pan. Cook over indirect heat for 2 hours. Baste with heated mixture of butter, orange juice and parsley. Cook over indirect heat for 2 hours longer or until cooked through, basting with heated mixture every 30 minutes.

Betsy White

SMOKED DUCK
Yield: 4 servings

	Hickory chips	1	teaspoon anise
1	(4- to 4½-pound) duckling	1	teaspoon garlic powder
1	teaspoon rosemary	1	teaspoon white pepper
1	teaspoon fennel	1	teaspoon paprika
		½	cup salt

Soak hickory chips in water for 30 minutes or longer. Rinse duckling and pat dry. Combine rosemary, fennel, anise, garlic powder, white pepper, paprika and salt in bowl; mix well. Reserve 1 tablespoon of rosemary mixture. Rub remaining mixture evenly over outside of duck; sprinkle reserved rosemary mixture inside body cavity. Drain hickory chips; sprinkle over hot coals. Smoke duck at 200° F to 225° F over indirect heat for 2½ hours or until legs move freely and internal temperature in thigh reaches 160° F to 165° F on meat thermometer.

*Rich Davis & Shifra Stein, co-authors of **All About B-B-Q: Kansas City-Style***

BOBO FAMILY BARBEQUED RABBIT

Yield: 8 servings

2	rabbits, cut into quarters	1	clove of garlic, minced
1	cup vegetable oil		Juice of ½ lemon
5	tablespoons catsup	1	teaspoon celery salt
¼	cup vinegar	¼	teaspoon pepper
¼	cup red wine	⅛	teaspoon cayenne
¼	cup A.1. steak sauce	4	drops of Tabasco sauce
1	small onion, minced		

Rinse rabbits and pat dry. Combine oil, catsup, vinegar, red wine, steak sauce, onion, garlic, lemon juice, celery salt, pepper, cayenne and Tabasco sauce in saucepan; mix well. Simmer for 20 minutes, stirring frequently. Baste rabbit quarters generously with sauce. Grill rabbit over hot coals for 30 to 40 minutes or until cooked through, turning and basting heavily with sauce every 5 minutes.

Vince Staten, **Jack Daniel's Old Time Barbecue Cookbook**

'Que Tip

Soak wood chips or chunks in water for at
least thirty minutes before using. Use dry oak to
keep fire up to correct temperature. Use hickory,
apple, or peach for a sweet mellow taste.

GRILLED RABBIT

Yield: 6 servings

1	(6-ounce) can frozen apple juice concentrate, thawed	2	teaspoons cornstarch
¼	cup packed brown sugar	2	(to 4) tablespoons cold water
¼	cup catsup	1	(2- to 2½-pound) rabbit
1	tablespoon vinegar		Salt and pepper to taste
½	teaspoon thyme	1	(to 2) tablespoons
	Hot pepper sauce to taste		vegetable oil

Combine apple juice concentrate, brown sugar, catsup, vinegar, thyme and hot pepper sauce in saucepan; mix well. Cook until brown sugar dissolves, stirring frequently. Stir in mixture of cornstarch and cold water. Cook until thickened, stirring constantly. Set aside. Rinse rabbit and pat dry. Sprinkle with salt and pepper. Arrange rabbit bone side up on grill rack. Grill over medium-hot coals for 20 minutes. Brush with oil; turn rabbit. Grill for 10 minutes. Brush with apple juice sauce. Grill for 10 minutes longer, turning and basting with apple juice sauce after 5 minutes.

Brenda Tunstill, Tunstill's Hot Off The Grill

This recipe earned Brenda Tunstill a first place ribbon at the Missouri State Fair.

'Que Tip

Hot coals are barely covered with a gray ash. **Medium** coals glow through the layer of gray ash. **Low** coals are covered with a thick layer of gray ash.

BARBEQUED VENISON
Yield: 6 servings

1	(3-pound) venison roast Morton Nature's Seasons Seasoning Blend to taste	3	tablespoons Worcestershire sauce
3/4	cup red wine vinegar	1 1/2	tablespoons garlic salt
3/4	cup vegetable oil	1 1/2	teaspoons dry mustard
3/4	cup catsup		Pepper to taste
		1	cup (or more) barbeque sauce

Sprinkle roast with Nature's seasoning. Pour mixture of wine vinegar, oil, catsup, Worcestershire sauce, garlic salt, dry mustard and pepper over roast in nonreactive dish, turning to coat. Marinate, covered, in refrigerator for 8 hours or longer. Drain, reserving marinade. Arrange hot coals around sides of covered grill and allow to burn down for 45 minutes. Place roast in center of grill. Cook with lid down for 30 minutes, turning every 5 minutes to sear. Cook at 225° F for 1 1/2 hours, turning every 15 to 20 minutes and basting occasionally with reserved marinade. Cook for 30 minutes longer, turning every 5 minutes and basting frequently with barbeque sauce.

*Rich Davis & Shifra Stein, co-authors of **All About B-B-Q: Kansas City-Style***

'Que Tip
If using a gas barbeque, you can grill roasts
evenly, without flare-ups, by turning on heat on one
side of the barbeque unit and placing the roast over a
drip pan on the other side.

GRILLED DEER TENDERLOIN

Yield: 2 servings

2	aged deer filets mignons	Thyme to taste
	Beef base	Garlic powder to taste
¼	teaspoon (about) brown sugar	Onion powder to taste
	Freshly ground Pepper Royale to taste	

Rub both sides of filets with a small amount of beef base. Let stand until meat starts to sweat. Rub both sides with brown sugar; sprinkle with Pepper Royale, thyme, garlic powder and onion powder. Grill filets over hot coals until medium-rare, turning occasionally; do not overcook. Pepper Royale is a mixture of white, red, black and green peppercorns. May substitute whole deer tenderloin, trimmed, butterflied and wrapped in bacon for filets.

Jim Burnett, Smoke-E-Holics

Jim Burnett of the Smoke-E-Holics won the National Wildlife Cook-Off for three consecutive years.

'Que Tip

Meat should be allowed to rest for at least fifteen to twenty minutes before carving.

GRILLED VENISON STEAK

Yield: 6 servings

½ cup soy sauce	4 (or 5) fresh basil leaves, crushed
¼ cup pepper vinegar	
¼ cup dry red wine	2 (to 3) tablespoons sugar
3 cloves of garlic, minced	1 (1½- to 2-pound) deer round steak

Pour mixture of soy sauce, pepper vinegar, red wine, garlic, basil and sugar over venison in sealable plastic bag; seal bag. Marinate in refrigerator for 8 hours or longer, turning occasionally. Drain steak, discarding marinade. Grill over hot coals for 3 to 5 minutes per side for rare or until done to taste. Remove to serving platter; cut into strips. May substitute elk for deer.

Karen Adler

Karen Adler not only cooks wild game, but she is an accomplished hunter. Dinner guests are often surprised and delighted with her game offerings.

VENISON BURGERS ITALIA

Yield: 4 servings

1 pound ground venison	¼ cup grated Romano cheese
½ white onion, finely chopped	
	1½ teaspoons oregano
1 cup spaghetti sauce	Salt and pepper to taste

Combine ground venison, onion, ⅓ cup of the spaghetti sauce, cheese, oregano, salt and pepper in bowl; mix well. Shape into four 1-inch thick patties. Grill over hot coals for 4 to 5 minutes. Turn and brush with remaining spaghetti sauce. Grill until done to taste. Serve with Italian-style salad, garlic toast and chianti.

Karen Adler

MARINADES, RUBS & SAUCES

❦

Seasonings, which may be achieved in different ways, come in several varieties. One is a marinade that is a liquid, usually with acid base of vinegar or wine, spices and oil, in which meat is soaked prior to cooking. Another is a rub or blend of dry spices added to the meat prior to cooking. A cross between the rub and marinade is the paste, a thick mixture of spices in a small amount of liquid that may be spread on the meat. A baste, usually reserved marinade, imparts flavor to the meat. Finally, there's the sauce. If using a sauce with tomatoes and sugar or molasses, apply to meat during the last fifteen to twenty minutes of cooking. Otherwise, it will be a burned sticky mess. If preferred, serve the sauce as a condiment at the table.

BEER MARINADE

Yield: 2¹/₄ cups

1	(12-ounce) can premium beer	¹/₄	cup salad oil
¹/₄	cup packed dark brown sugar	3	bay leaves
		1	teaspoon salt
		¹/₂	teaspoon pepper

Combine beer, brown sugar, salad oil, bay leaves, salt and pepper in bowl, stirring until brown sugar dissolves. Use as marinade and/or basting sauce.

Paul Kirk, K.C. Baron of Barbecue

BURGUNDY MARINADE

Yield: 3 1/2 cups

1 (25-ounce) bottle burgundy	2 cloves of garlic, crushed
1/2 cup chopped onion	2 tablespoons catsup
2 tablespoons Worcestershire sauce	2 tablespoons vegetable oil
2 tablespoons vinegar	1 teaspoon marjoram
	1/2 teaspoon rosemary

Combine burgundy, onion, Worcestershire sauce, vinegar, garlic, catsup, oil, marjoram and rosemary in bowl; mix well. Use as marinade and/or basting sauce.

Smoky Hale, **Smoky Hale's Great American Barbeque Instruction Book**

CIDER MINT MARINADE

Yield: 1 1/4 cups

1 cup sweet apple cider	1 teaspoon sea salt
1/2 cup cider vinegar	1/4 cup minced fresh mint leaves
1 tablespoon clover honey	

Bring apple cider and cider vinegar to a boil in saucepan; reduce heat. Stir in honey and sea salt. Simmer over medium heat for 10 minutes, stirring occasionally. Stir in mint. Simmer for 5 minutes longer, stirring occasionally. Use as marinade and/or basting sauce. Great with lamb.

Carolyn Wells

'Que Tip

If serving leftover marinade as an accompaniment, be sure to boil marinade before serving to kill any food-borne microorganisms.

DIRTY DICK'S POULTRY MARINADE

Yield: 1 cup

½	cup butter	1	teaspoon oregano
½	cup lemon juice	1	teaspoon thyme
3	cloves of garlic, crushed	1	teaspoon salt
1	tablespoon brown sugar	½	teaspoon pepper
1	tablespoon minced fresh	¼	teaspoon cayenne
	tarragon	5	sprigs of fresh rosemary

Combine butter, lemon juice, garlic, brown sugar, tarragon, oregano, thyme, salt, pepper, cayenne and rosemary in saucepan. Cook over low heat until butter melts, stirring frequently. Pour over poultry in non-reactive dish, turning to coat. Marinate in refrigerator for 8 hours or longer. Grill poultry over hot coals until cooked through, basting with remaining marinade frequently.

Richard Westhaver, Dirty Dick's Legless Wonders

POULTRY MARINADE

Yield: 2 cups

½	cup Mongolian Fire oil	1	teaspoon dry mustard
½	cup sesame oil	½	teaspoon ground ginger
½	cup soy sauce	½	cup white wine

Combine Mongolian Fire oil, sesame oil, soy sauce, dry mustard, ginger and white wine in jar with tightfitting lid; shake to mix. Pour over poultry in nonreactive dish, turning to coat. Marinate in refrigerator for 1 hour or longer, turning occasionally. Grill or smoke until cooked through.

Rich & Bunny Tuttle, K-Cass Bar-B-Que

GAME MARINADE

Yield: 2¼ cups

1	cup vinegar	2	whole cloves
1	cup water	1	clove of garlic, crushed
2	medium onions, sliced	1	teaspoon salt
	Juice of 1 lemon	1	teaspoon pepper
2	bay leaves	½	teaspoon tarragon

Combine vinegar, water, onions, lemon juice, bay leaves, cloves, garlic, salt, pepper and tarragon in bowl; mix well. Use as marinade and/or basting sauce for game. May substitute cranberry juice for vinegar.

*Smoky Hale, **Smoky Hale's Great American Barbeque Instruction Book***

LAMB MARINADE & SAUCE

Yield: 1 cup

¾	cup sherry	1	sprig of parsley
2	tablespoons olive oil	1	sprig of fresh rosemary or
1	teaspoon grated onion		½ teaspoon dried
1	teaspoon salt		rosemary
½	teaspoon pepper	1	sprig of fresh oregano or
1	lemon slice		½ teaspoon dried oregano

Combine sherry, olive oil, onion, salt, pepper, lemon slice, parsley, rosemary and oregano in bowl; mix well. Let stand at room temperature for several hours to allow flavors to blend. Use as marinade and/or basting sauce for lamb. May heat and serve with lamb.

Donna McClure, P.D.T. (Pretty Damn Tasty)

ORIENTAL HOISIN MARINADE
Yield: 1 1/2 cups

4	cloves of garlic, minced	1/3	cup soy sauce
2	teaspoons grated gingerroot	3	tablespoons dry red wine
1/2	cup hoisin sauce	2	tablespoons Oriental chili sauce
1/3	cup honey, at room temperature	1	teaspoon salt

Combine garlic and gingerroot in bowl; mix well. Stir in hoisin sauce, honey, soy sauce, red wine, chili sauce and salt. Use as marinade and/or basting sauce.

Paul Kirk, K.C. Baron of Barbecue

PIGSKIN PETE'S PORK MARINADE
Yield: 2 cups

1/2	cup honey	1/4	cup soy sauce
1/2	cup cranberry juice	2	tablespoons cranberry preserves
1/4	cup prepared mustard		
1/4	cup Worcestershire sauce	1	tablespoon favorite barbeque rub
1/4	cup A.1. steak sauce		

Combine honey, cranberry juice, mustard, Worcestershire sauce, steak sauce, soy sauce, cranberry preserves and barbeque rub in bowl; mix well. Pour over pork in nonreactive dish. Marinate in refrigerator for 8 hours or longer, turning occasionally. Grill or smoke pork, basting with marinade frequently.

Richard Westhaver, Dirty Dick's Legless Wonders

'Que Tip
Use leftover marinade as a basting sauce.

SESAME GINGER MARINADE

Yield: 2 cups

½ cup light soy sauce	2 tablespoons grated gingerroot
½ cup garlic vinegar	
½ cup sesame oil	2 cloves of garlic, crushed
½ cup canola oil	1 teaspoon pepper

Mix soy sauce, garlic vinegar, sesame oil, canola oil, gingerroot, garlic and pepper in bowl. Use as marinade and/or basting sauce.

Paul Kirk, K.C. Baron of Barbecue

TERIYAKI MARINADE & SAUCE

Yield: 1¼ cups

½ cup soy sauce	1 clove of garlic, crushed
½ cup lemon juice	½ teaspoon ground ginger
¼ cup olive oil	

Combine soy sauce, lemon juice, olive oil, garlic and ginger in bowl; mix well. Use as marinade and/or basting sauce.

Ardie Davis

VINAIGRETTE MARINADE

Yield: 1 cup

½ cup vegetable oil	2 tablespoons sugar
⅓ cup lemon juice or vinegar	2 cloves of garlic, crushed
¼ cup minced green onions	2 teaspoons beef bouillon granules
2 tablespoons Dijon mustard	

Combine all ingredients in bowl, stirring until bouillon dissolves. Use as marinade and/or basting sauce.

Betsy White

BARBEQUE RUB
Yield: 2½ cups

1 cup sugar	2 tablespoons pepper
½ cup salt	2 tablespoons garlic powder
¼ cup celery salt	1 tablespoon chili powder
3 tablespoons paprika	1 teaspoon savory
2 tablespoons barbeque spice	½ teaspoon cayenne

Combine sugar, salt, celery salt, paprika, barbeque spice, pepper, garlic powder, chili powder, savory and cayenne in bowl; mix well. Rub liberally over entire surface of meat. Let stand at room temperature for up to 15 minutes or marinate in refrigerator for up to 24 hours. Store rub in airtight container.

Sheila Sneed

BARBEQUE BEEF RUB
Yield: 3 cups

1 cup sugar	1 teaspoon cumin
1 cup garlic salt	1 teaspoon onion powder
½ cup paprika	½ teaspoon cilantro
3 tablespoons pepper	
2 tablespoons chili seasoning	

Combine sugar, garlic salt, paprika, pepper, chili seasoning, cumin, onion powder and cilantro in bowl; mix well. Rub liberally over your favorite cut of beef. Let stand at room temperature for up to 15 minutes or marinate in refrigerator for up to 24 hours. Store rub in airtight container.

Paul Kirk, K.C. Baron of Barbecue

BARBEQUE POULTRY RUB

Yield: 3 cups

½	cup garlic salt	2	tablespoons limeade mix
½	cup onion salt	1	tablespoon parsley flakes
½	cup maple sugar	1	teaspoon cayenne
½	cup cane sugar	½	teaspoon ground anise
½	cup paprika	½	teaspoon ground ginger
2	tablespoons lemon pepper	½	teaspoon cinnamon
2	tablespoons granulated garlic		

Combine garlic salt, onion salt, maple sugar, cane sugar, paprika, lemon pepper, garlic, limeade mix, parsley flakes, cayenne, anise, ginger and cinnamon in bowl; mix well. Rub liberally over poultry. Store rub in airtight container. May purchase maple sugar at health food stores.

Bill Cupito, Powderpuff Barbeque

BARBEQUE PORK RUB

Yield: 3 cups

1	cup packed dark brown sugar	2	tablespoons black pepper
1	cup celery salt	1	tablespoon lemon pepper
½	cup paprika	1	teaspoon garlic powder
3	tablespoons chili powder	½	teaspoon cinnamon
		¼	teaspoon cayenne

Combine brown sugar, celery salt, paprika, chili powder, black pepper, lemon pepper, garlic powder, cinnamon and cayenne in bowl; mix well. Rub liberally over your favorite cut of pork. Let stand at room temperature for up to 15 minutes or marinate in refrigerator for up to 24 hours. Store rub in airtight container.

John Harvey

BARBEQUE SEASONING
Yield: 2 1/2 cups

1 cup salt	1 teaspoon ground celery seeds
1 cup sugar	
1/4 cup paprika	1 teaspoon crushed rosemary
1 teaspoon white pepper	
1 teaspoon chili seasoning	1/2 teaspoon dillweed
1 teaspoon garlic powder	1/4 teaspoon ground bay leaf

Combine salt, sugar, paprika, white pepper, chili seasoning, garlic powder, celery seeds, rosemary, dillweed and bay leaf in bowl; mix well. Rub liberally over entire surface of meat. Let stand at room temperature for up to 15 minutes or marinate in refrigerator for up to 24 hours. Store rub in airtight container. May add 1/4 teaspoon MSG.

Pierce Walker

BROWN SUGAR RUB
Yield: 2 cups

1 cup packed dark brown sugar	1 tablespoon dry mustard
	1 tablespoon allspice
1/2 cup celery salt	1/2 teaspoon ground cloves
1/2 cup onion salt	

Spread brown sugar on baking sheet. Air-dry for 3 to 5 hours, stirring every hour. Sift dried brown sugar into bowl. Stir in celery salt, onion salt, dry mustard, allspice and cloves. Rub liberally over entire surface of meat. Let stand at room temperature for up to 15 minutes or marinate in refrigerator for up to 24 hours. Store rub in airtight container. May add 1/2 teaspoon MSG.

Monty Spradling, Voo Doo BBQ

CRISPY CRITTER DRY RUB & BASTING SAUCE

Yield: 3¾ cups

1½ cups paprika

½ cup black pepper

½ cup garlic salt

½ cup white pepper

½ cup salt

¼ cup rubbed sage

Combine paprika, black pepper, garlic salt, white pepper, salt and sage in bowl; mix well. Rub pork shoulder or whole hog with mixture just before barbequing. Combine 2 cups of the dry rub with 1 gallon boiling vinegar for basting sauce.

Skip Gigliotti, Crispy Critters

HOT-OFF-THE-GRILL RUB

Yield: 1 cup

¼ cup Hungarian paprika

2 tablespoons salt

2 tablespoons sugar

2 tablespoons brown sugar

2 tablespoons cumin

2 tablespoons chili powder

2 tablespoons freshly ground pepper

1 tablespoon cayenne

Combine paprika, salt, sugar, brown sugar, cumin, chili powder, pepper and cayenne in bowl; mix well. Rub liberally over entire surface of meat. Let stand at room temperature for up to 15 minutes or marinate in refrigerator for up to 24 hours. Store rub in airtight container.

Brenda Tunstill, Tunstill's Hot Off the Grill

'Que Tip

Beef, pork, lamb, and chicken all benefit from being marinated for a few hours to overnight.

HICKORY BARBEQUE RUB

Yield: 3 cups

1 cup sugar	¼ cup barbeque spice
⅓ cup garlic salt	¼ cup chili powder
⅓ cup onion salt	¼ cup pepper
⅓ cup hickory salt	1 teaspoon cayenne
⅓ cup paprika	

Combine sugar, garlic salt, onion salt, hickory salt, paprika, barbeque spice, chili powder, pepper and cayenne in bowl; mix well. Rub liberally over entire surface of meat. Let stand at room temperature for up to 15 minutes or marinate in refrigerator for up to 24 hours. Store rub in airtight container. May add 1 teaspoon MSG.

Ardie Davis

K-CASS DRY RUB

Yield: 1¼ cups

1 cup packed dark brown sugar	1 teaspoon cayenne
1½ tablespoons celery salt	1 teaspoon salt
1 tablespoon paprika	½ teaspoon pepper
2 teaspoons dry mustard	¼ teaspoon garlic powder
	¼ teaspoon onion powder

Spread brown sugar on baking sheet. Air-dry for about 2 hours, stirring every 30 to 45 minutes. Sift dried brown sugar into bowl. Stir in celery salt, paprika, dry mustard, cayenne, salt, pepper, garlic powder and onion powder. Use as rub on pork chops, roasts, chicken, ribs and brisket. Store rub in airtight container.

Rich & Bunny Tuttle, K-Cass Bar-B-Que

KANSAS CITY RIB RUB

Yield: 2¹/₂ cups

1 cup cane sugar	2 tablespoons chili seasoning
¹/₃ cup paprika	2 tablespoons black pepper
¹/₄ cup seasoned salt	1 tablespoon lemon pepper
¹/₄ cup garlic salt	2 teaspoons ground ginger
¹/₄ cup celery salt	¹/₂ teaspoon thyme
2 tablespoons onion salt	¹/₂ teaspoon allspice
2 tablespoons barbeque seasoning	¹/₂ teaspoon cayenne

Sift cane sugar, paprika, seasoned salt, garlic salt, celery salt, onion salt, barbeque seasoning, chili seasoning, black pepper, lemon pepper, ginger, thyme, allspice and cayenne into bowl; mix well. Rub liberally over ribs. Let stand at room temperature for up to 15 minutes or marinate in refrigerator for up to 24 hours. Store rub in airtight container in cool place.

Paul Kirk, K.C. Baron of Barbecue

POWDERPUFF RIB RUB

Yield: 1 cup

¹/₂ cup celery salt	2 tablespoons ground pepper
¹/₄ cup granulated garlic	
¹/₄ cup paprika	

Combine celery salt, garlic, paprika and pepper in bowl; mix well. Spray baby back ribs with nonstick cooking spray; rub liberally with mixture. Smoke ribs until cooked through.

Janeyce Michel-Cupito, Powderpuff Barbeque

SPICY BARBEQUE RUB
Yield: 2¾ cups

½   cup packed light brown sugar
½   cup sugar
½   cup garlic salt
½   cup paprika
3   tablespoons seasoned salt
1   tablespoon celery salt
¼   cup chili powder

3   tablespoons black pepper
1   tablespoon lemon pepper
1   tablespoon ground red pepper
½   teaspoon allspice
½   teaspoon oregano
½   teaspoon savory

Combine brown sugar, sugar, garlic salt, paprika, seasoned salt, celery salt, chili powder, black pepper, lemon pepper, red pepper, allspice, oregano and savory in bowl; mix well. Rub liberally over entire surface of meat. Let stand at room temperature for up to 15 minutes or marinate in refrigerator for up to 24 hours. May add 2 teaspoons MSG to rub.

Ardie Davis

TNT RUB
Yield: 3 cups

2   cups sugar
½   cup salt
¼   cup paprika
2   tablespoons black pepper
2   tablespoons chili powder

2   teaspoons cayenne
2   teaspoons dry mustard
1   teaspoon cinnamon
    Red pepper to taste

Combine sugar, salt, paprika, black pepper, chili powder, cayenne, dry mustard, cinnamon and red pepper in bowl; mix well. Rub pork or poultry liberally with rub. Marinate in refrigerator for 2 to 8 hours, turning occasionally. Barbeque until cooked through.

Harold Jansen, Tap and Trawf Kookers

APPLE CITY SAUCE

Yield: 2 cups

1   cup catsup
¼   cup soy sauce
¼   cup cider vinegar
¼   cup apple juice
2   tablespoons
      Worcestershire sauce
¼   medium onion, finely
      grated

2   teaspoons grated green
      bell pepper
¾   teaspoon granulated garlic
¾   teaspoon ground white
      pepper
      Sugar to taste
¼   Golden Delicious apple,
      peeled, grated

Combine first 10 ingredients in saucepan; mix well. Simmer over low heat for 5 to 10 minutes or until of the desired consistency, stirring occasionally. Stir in apple. Simmer for 5 minutes longer. Use as a finishing sauce and table sauce with any cut of pork, especially ribs. Store in refrigerator for up to 1 week.

Jim Auchmutey & Susan Puckett, **The Ultimate Barbecue Sauce Cookbook,** *Longstreet Press*

BARBEQUE BASTING SAUCE

Yield: 1½ cups

1   cup peanut oil
½   cup soy sauce
1   tablespoon salt
1   tablespoon seasoned salt

2   bay leaves
      Juice and sliced rind of
      4 lemons

Combine all ingredients in saucepan; mix well. Simmer for 3 to 5 minutes or until of the desired consistency, stirring frequently. Discard lemon rind and bay leaves. Use as a basting sauce for grilled chicken. This recipe makes enough sauce to baste 5 chickens.

Melody Morgan, Vienna Volunteer Fire Department Cooking Team

---

*The Vienna Volunteer Fire Department team members are
consistent winners on the Memphis in May circuit.*

BARBEQUE SAUCE

Yield: 2½ cups

¾ cup crushed pineapple
½ cup catsup
½ cup water
¼ cup chopped onion
3 tablespoons salad oil
2 tablespoons brown sugar
2 tablespoons lemon juice
2 tablespoons wine vinegar
2 tablespoons soy sauce

1 tablespoon prepared mustard
1 teaspoon salt
1 teaspoon Worcestershire sauce
½ teaspoon ground ginger
¼ teaspoon Tabasco sauce
⅛ teaspoon garlic powder

Bring pineapple, catsup, water, onion, salad oil, brown sugar, lemon juice, wine vinegar, soy sauce, mustard, salt, Worcestershire sauce, ginger, Tabasco sauce and garlic powder to a boil in saucepan, stirring occasionally; reduce heat. Simmer for 5 minutes, stirring occasionally. Use to baste ribs.

Ernie Heimsoth, Chigger Creek

BARBEQUE DIPPING SAUCE

Yield: 2½ cups

2 cups catsup
½ cup apple cider vinegar
¼ cup packed light brown sugar

Juice of 1 lemon
Salt and pepper to taste

Combine catsup, vinegar, brown sugar, lemon juice, salt and pepper in saucepan; mix well. Simmer just until heated through, stirring occasionally. Serve hot or cold as dipping sauce for chicken or pork.

Steve Morgan, Vienna Volunteer Fire Department Cooking Team

HACKING SAUCE

Yield: 1³/4 cups

1 cup water	¹/₂ teaspoon cayenne
¹/₂ cup catsup	¹/₂ teaspoon brown sugar
¹/₃ cup apple cider vinegar	¹/₂ teaspoon Terpin
1 teaspoon chili powder	hydrate-D-M cough
1 teaspoon salt	syrup
1 teaspoon celery seeds	¹/₈ teaspoon nutmeg
¹/₂ teaspoon cinnamon	

Bring water, catsup, cider vinegar, chili powder, salt, celery seeds, cinnamon, cayenne, brown sugar, cough syrup and nutmeg to a boil in saucepan, stirring occasionally. Remove from heat. Cool slightly. Pour into bowl. Let stand, covered, in refrigerator for 5 days to allow flavors to marry.

Greg Johnson & Vince Staten, **Real Barbecue**

HOT PEPPER BASTING SAUCE

Yield: ³/4 cup

4 (to 5) jalapeños, seeded	2 tablespoons brown sugar
2 large green peppers, skinned, seeded	2 tablespoons vegetable oil
¹/₂ cup fresh lime juice	¹/₂ teaspoon cumin

Process jalapeños, green peppers, lime juice, brown sugar, oil and cumin in blender until puréed. Heat in saucepan just until warm. Use to baste shrimp, beef or chicken.

Chile Pepper

'Que Tip

Sauces may be made and stored, covered,
in the refrigerator for up to one week or frozen
for up to three months.

KANSAS CITY BASTING SAUCE

Yield: 5 cups

1½ cups cider vinegar	10 bay leaves
1½ cups apple juice	5 cloves of garlic
½ cup Worcestershire sauce	2 tablespoons dry mustard
½ cup teriyaki sauce	2 tablespoons Louisiana hot sauce
¼ cup catsup	
¼ cup margarine	2 teaspoons soy sauce
¼ cup corn syrup	1 teaspoon salt
¼ cup dark molasses	1 teaspoon oregano
1 onion, cut into quarters	1 teaspoon thyme
1 lemon, cut into quarters	1 teaspoon white pepper
16 whole cloves	½ teaspoon cayenne

Bring cider vinegar, apple juice, Worcestershire sauce, teriyaki sauce, catsup, margarine, corn syrup, molasses, onion, lemon, cloves, bay leaves, garlic, dry mustard, hot sauce, soy sauce, salt, oregano, thyme, white pepper and cayenne to a boil in heavy saucepan, stirring occasionally; reduce heat. Cook until onion is tender, stirring occasionally; strain. Use as desired for basting sauce.

Jim Burnett, Smoke-E-Holics

'Que Tip

Add honey, brown sugar, or molasses to
commercial barbeque sauce for a sweeter sauce or add
jalapeño juice for a spicier flavor. Allow one-half cup of
barbeque sauce for each pound of meat.

KANSAS CITY CLASSIC SAUCE
Yield: 4¹/₂ cups

³/₄ cup packed brown sugar	¹/₄ teaspoon ground red pepper
1 (to 2) tablespoons ground black pepper	¹/₄ teaspoon mace
1 (1-ounce) envelope chili seasoning	1 cup vinegar
2 teaspoons dry mustard	¹/₄ cup molasses
1 teaspoon ground ginger	¹/₄ cup water
¹/₂ teaspoon allspice	1 (32-ounce) bottle catsup

Combine brown sugar, black pepper, chili seasoning, dry mustard, ginger, allspice, red pepper and mace in saucepan; mix well. Add vinegar, molasses and water, stirring until blended. Stir in catsup. Bring to a boil, stirring constantly; reduce heat. Simmer, covered, over low heat for 30 minutes, stirring occasionally. Use as a finishing and table sauce for beef, pork and chicken or add to your favorite meat loaf recipe. May store sauce in refrigerator for several weeks. May add 1 to 3 teaspoons liquid smoke.

Jim Auchmutey & Susan Puckett, **The Ultimate Barbecue Sauce Cookbook***, Longstreet Press*

'Que Tip
"A pig in a poke" referred to a common trick in 17th century England of trying to palm off a cat for a suckling pig to an unsuspecting "greenhorn." When the poke (sack) was opened and the trick disclosed, the person duped "let the cat out of the bag."

KENTUCKY COLONEL SAUCE

Yield: 3 cups

2½	cups water	1	tablespoon salt
¼	cup vinegar	1	clove of garlic, minced
¼	cup chopped onion	2	teaspoons chili powder
3	tablespoons pepper	1	teaspoon cayenne
3	tablespoons Worcestershire sauce	1	teaspoon hot red pepper sauce
2	tablespoons butter	1	teaspoon dry mustard
1	tablespoon sugar		

Bring water, vinegar, onion, pepper, Worcestershire sauce, butter, sugar, salt, garlic, chili powder, cayenne, hot pepper sauce and dry mustard to a boil in saucepan; reduce heat. Simmer for 5 minutes, stirring occasionally. Let stand until cool. Chill, covered, for 8 hours or longer. Heat in saucepan until warm. Baste pork at beginning of cooking process and continue basting occasionally until internal temperature registers 170° F on meat thermometer.

Greg Johnson & Vince Staten, **Real Barbecue**

'Que Tip

When using barbeque sauce that does not contain sugar, apply the sauce every forty-five to sixty minutes. This prevents the meat from drying out during grilling or smoking. Barbeque sauce that contains sugar should be applied only during the last stages of grilling or smoking.

MICHAEL CONNER'S "BLACK MAGIC" BARBEQUE SAUCE

Yield: 4 cups

½ small onion, finely chopped
1 tablespoon vegetable oil
1 clove of garlic, minced
¼ cup packed brown sugar
1¼ cups catsup
½ cup apple cider vinegar
½ cup Creole mustard

¼ cup dark beer
2 tablespoons blackstrap molasses
2 tablespoons Worcestershire sauce
1 tablespoon liquid smoke
1 teaspoon Tabasco sauce
½ teaspoon cayenne

Sauté onion in oil in saucepan over high heat until tender. Add garlic and brown sugar; mix well; reduce heat. Cook until brown sugar melts and darkens, stirring constantly. Stir in catsup, cider vinegar, Creole mustard, beer, molasses, Worcestershire sauce, liquid smoke, Tabasco sauce and cayenne. Simmer over low heat for 30 minutes, stirring occasionally. Serve as an accompaniment to smoked meats.

*Paris Permenter & John Bigley, co-authors of **Texas Barbecue***

MOP SAUCE

Yield: 4 cups

2 cups beef stock
1 cup beer
⅔ cup Worcestershire sauce
⅓ cup vegetable oil
1½ teaspoons salt
1½ teaspoons dry mustard
1½ teaspoons paprika

1 teaspoon garlic powder
1 teaspoon chili powder
1 teaspoon Louisiana hot sauce
½ teaspoon black pepper
½ teaspoon red pepper

Combine all ingredients in bowl; mix well. Use as mopping sauce on desired cuts of meat. May store leftover sauce in refrigerator.

Merle Ellis, The Butcher

MOPPIN' SAUCE
Yield: 3 cups

2 cups beef stock	1½ teaspoons paprika
½ cup melted butter	1 teaspoon freshly ground
¼ cup vegetable oil	pepper
¼ cup fresh lemon juice	1 teaspoon garlic powder
1 tablespoon Worcestershire	1 teaspoon Louisiana hot
sauce	sauce
2 teaspoons chili powder	½ teaspoon salt

Combine stock, butter, oil, lemon juice, Worcestershire sauce, chili powder, paprika, pepper, garlic powder, hot sauce and salt in bowl; mix well. Use as mop on desired cuts of meat.

Bill Robinson, Fire N' Smoke

BASIC MOPPING SAUCE
Yield: 2½ cups

1 cup strong coffee	1 tablespoon freshly ground
½ cup Worcestershire sauce	pepper
1 cup catsup	1 tablespoon sugar
¼ cup unsalted butter	1 tablespoon salt

Combine coffee, Worcestershire sauce, catsup, butter, pepper, sugar and salt in saucepan; mix well. Simmer for 30 minutes, stirring frequently. Use as mop for beef or poultry. May store sauce in refrigerator and reheat before using.

Ardie Davis & Barbara Ginsterblum

'Que Tip
When making your own sauce, be sure to cook the sauce uncovered so it will reduce to desired consistency.

WILDMAN'S POULTRY MOP

Yield: 2½ cups

1	(12-ounce) can flat beer, at room temperature	1	tablespoon Tabasco sauce
½	cup melted butter	1	tablespoon barbeque rub
½	cup vegetable oil	1	teaspoon poultry seasoning
2	tablespoons lemon juice	¼	teaspoon basil

Combine beer, butter, oil, lemon juice, Tabasco sauce, barbeque rub, poultry seasoning and basil in saucepan; mix well. Simmer for 10 minutes, stirring occasionally. Use as baste for poultry. May add ½ teaspoon MSG to mop.

Barry Martin, Wildman's BBQ

MUSHROOM SAUCE FOR STEAK

Yield: 3 cups

1	pound fresh mushrooms, sliced	½	cup unsalted butter
		2	cups whipping cream

Sauté mushrooms in butter in skillet over medium heat for 2 minutes. Add whipping cream; mix well. Bring to a boil, stirring constantly. Bring to a rolling boil, stirring occasionally. Boil until mixture is reduced by ½. Serve with your favorite steak.

Carolyn Wells

'Que Tip

Barbeque sauce may be used to marinate meat and vegetables. Marinate in a noncorrosive container in the refrigerator, turning meat and/or vegetables occasionally.

POWDERPUFF BARBEQUE SAUCE

Yield: 5 cups

1	(18-ounce) can tomato paste	4	cloves of garlic, minced
1	(10-ounce) can tomatoes with green chiles, puréed	2	tablespoons chili powder
		1	tablespoon salt
1	cup cider vinegar	1	tablespoon ground pepper
1	cup molasses	1	tablespoon paprika
1	cup packed brown sugar	1	teaspoon celery seeds
1	medium onion, finely minced	1	teaspoon dry mustard
		1	teaspoon Louisiana hot pepper sauce

Bring tomato paste and remaining ingredients just to boiling point in saucepan; reduce heat. Simmer for 1 hour, stirring occasionally. May omit tomatoes with green chiles for milder sauce.

Janeyce Michel-Cupito, Powderpuff Barbeque

PRIVATE STOCK STEAK SAUCE

Yield: 1 3/4 cups

1/2	cup finely minced onion	1	tablespoon pepper
2	cloves of garlic, minced	1 1/2	teaspoons dry mustard
2	cups butter	1	teaspoon salt
1/2	cup whiskey	1/4	teaspoon Tabasco sauce
1/4	cup Worcestershire sauce		

Sauté onion and garlic in butter in saucepan until onion is tender. Stir in remaining ingredients. Use to baste sirloin steak, 1 1/2 to 2 inches thick. Grill over hot coals until done to taste. Cut diagonally into 1/2-inch slices. Reheat remaining sauce in saucepan; spoon over steak.

Hoelting Brothers

The Hoelting Brothers of Shawnee, Kansas, are past Grand Champions of the American Royal/KC Masterpiece International Invitational Barbecue Contest. They are a very family-oriented team and world-class cookers.

ROASTED RED PEPPER VELVET

Yield: 2 cups

2   large red bell peppers
1½ cups corn oil
1   egg, at room temperature
2   tablespoons fresh lemon
    juice
1   teaspoon red wine
    vinegar

1½ tablespoons Dijon
    mustard
1   teaspoon salt
½   teaspoon freshly ground
    pepper
¾   teaspoon (or more)
    Tabasco sauce

Grill red peppers over medium heat until skin blisters and chars, turning every 1 to 2 minutes. Place peppers in saucepan. Let stand, covered, for 10 minutes or until skin can be removed easily with sharp knife. Set aside. Process 3 tablespoons of the corn oil, egg, lemon juice, red wine vinegar, Dijon mustard, salt, pepper and Tabasco sauce in food processor fitted with steel blade for 5 seconds or until blended. Add remaining corn oil gradually, processing constantly until thickened. Add red peppers. Process just until red peppers are coarsely chopped. Serve with vegetables, seafood, poultry and veal. May substitute ½ cup bottled coarsely chopped roasted red peppers, drained and dried on paper towels, for the fresh red peppers. May substitute pimento for red pepper.

Leslie Beal Bloom, **Barbecue Sizzling Fireside Know-How**

'Que Tip

Baste steaks and chops with barbeque sauce after
being turned for the last time or during the last three
minutes of grilling. Baste chicken with sauce
during the last ten minutes of grilling, turning once.
Hot dogs and sausage should be basted during the
last five to six minutes of cooking.

HOT & SWEET STRAWBERRY BARBEQUE SAUCE

Yield: 2 cups

2   cups sliced fresh strawberries

⅓   cup strawberry preserves

⅓   cup catsup

1   green onion, minced

2   tablespoons soy sauce

2   tablespoons lemon juice

2   tablespoons chopped fresh cilantro

1   large clove of garlic, minced

1   teaspoon chopped gingerroot

½   teaspoon grated lemon rind

¼   teaspoon cayenne

Process strawberries, strawberry preserves, catsup, green onion, soy sauce, lemon juice, cilantro, garlic, gingerroot, lemon rind and cayenne in blender until puréed. Use to marinate meat, fish or mushrooms and as basting sauce during grilling process. May simmer puréed mixture in saucepan until thickened and use as baste for ribs, chicken or steak.

Roxanne E. Chan, **Chile Pepper**

'Que Tip

Hot dogs, along with ice cream cones, were first introduced to the public at the St. Louis World's Fair in 1904. When hot dogs were first sold, street vendors called them "red hots," and they did not come on a bun. Instead, a pair of white cotton gloves came with each hot dog to keep fingers cool while eating.

WHISKEYQUE, TOO RECIPE

Yield: 1 1/2 gallons

9	cups Worcestershire sauce	1/2	cup pepper
8	cups catsup	1/2	cup salt
4	cups apple cider vinegar	1/2	cup minced garlic
2	cups packed brown sugar	6	tablespoons onion powder
2	cups sugar		Liquid smoke to taste
1 1/2	cups tomato juice	1	cup Jack Daniel's whiskey
1/2	cup Tabasco sauce		
1/2	cup paprika		

Combine Worcestershire sauce, catsup, apple cider vinegar, brown sugar, sugar, tomato juice, Tabasco sauce, paprika, pepper, salt, garlic, onion powder and liquid smoke in large saucepan; mix well. Simmer for 1 hour, stirring occasionally. Remove from heat. Let stand until cool. Stir in whiskey. Use as desired.

*Vince Staten, **Jack Daniel's Old Time Barbecue Cookbook***

EDSEL BUTTER

Yield: 1 cup

1	cup unsalted butter, softened	1	teaspoon Worcestershire sauce
2	tablespoons finely chopped drained pimento	1	teaspoon minced garlic
2	tablespoons chopped fresh chives	1/2	teaspoon onion salt

Beat butter in mixer bowl until creamy. Stir in pimento, chives, Worcestershire sauce, garlic and onion salt gently. Spoon into crock or covered glass bowl. Great on sourdough bread and a multitude of other foods. Store in refrigerator for up to 5 days. Let stand at room temperature for 1 hour before serving.

Art & Ardie Davis

VERSATILE BUTTER

Yield: 2 cups

1 **pound unsalted butter, softened**	¼ **cup buttermilk**

Beat butter in mixer bowl at low speed until whipped. Beat at high speed for 5 minutes longer, scraping bowl occasionally. Add buttermilk gradually, beating constantly at low speed until blended. Beat at high speed for 10 minutes longer or until light and fluffy, scraping bowl occasionally. Try these variations by blending ¾ cup of the whipped butter with the following ingredients.

• For **Honey Butter** add 2 tablespoons honey and ¼ teaspoon mace.

• For **Raspberry Butter** add ¼ cup mashed raspberries, 1 tablespoon confectioners' sugar and ⅛ teaspoon lemon juice.

• For **Orange Butter** add 1 tablespoon orange juice and ¼ teaspoon nutmeg.

• For **Barbeque Butter** add 2 tablespoons barbeque sauce, ¼ teaspoon lemon juice and ⅛ teaspoon cayenne.

• For **Spicy Butter** add 1 teaspoon garlic juice, ¼ teaspoon lemon juice and ¼ teaspoon celery seeds.

• For **Nutty Butter** add 3 tablespoons finely chopped pecans or any type of nuts.

Use these butters as flavor enhancers for all types of foods.

Paul Kirk, K.C. Baron of Barbecue

Chef Paul's latest venture is a barbeque instruction video.

COMPLEMENTS
FROM THE
CHEF

APPETIZERS

∽∽∽

ARTICHOKE DIP
Yield: 15 servings

2	(14-ounce) cans artichokes, drained, chopped	1	(4-ounce) can chopped black olives
2	cups freshly grated Parmesan cheese	1	cup mayonnaise
		1	teaspoon garlic powder
			Paprika to taste

Combine artichokes, cheese, olives, mayonnaise and garlic powder in bowl; mix well. Spoon into shallow baking dish; sprinkle with paprika. Bake at 325° F for 30 minutes. Serve hot with assorted party crackers.

Melody Morgan, Vienna Volunteer Fire Department Cooking Team

Melody Morgan is a member of the Vienna Volunteer Fire Department Cooking Team of Vienna, Georgia. They have won the Big Pig Jig, a 100-plus team contest, in Vienna on several occasions.

'Que Tip
Marinated meat should be wiped dry
before sprinkling with spices.

POTATO DIP

Yield: 50 servings

3	cups mashed potatoes	1½	teaspoons salt
2	cups 50% reduced-fat mayonnaise	½	teaspoon cayenne
⅓	cup fresh lime juice	¼	cup olive oil
3	tablespoons prepared horseradish	¼	cup minced green onions
1	tablespoon minced garlic	¼	cup minced carrot
2	teaspoons cumin	¼	cup minced red bell pepper

Place potatoes, mayonnaise, lime juice and horseradish in food processor or blender container; set aside. Sauté garlic, cumin, salt and cayenne in olive oil in skillet over medium-low heat for 3 minutes, stirring constantly. Add to potato mixture. Process until blended. Stir in green onions, carrot and red pepper. Serve hot or cold with chips and assorted fresh vegetables.

Rich Davis, K.C. Masterpiece BBQ & Grill

TEXAS CAVIAR

Yield: 15 servings

1	(23-ounce) can black-eyed peas, drained, rinsed	1	medium onion, chopped
1	(4-ounce) can diced mild or hot green chiles	¼	cup olive oil
		¼	cup white vinegar

Combine peas, green chiles, onion, olive oil and vinegar in bowl; mix well. Marinate, covered, in refrigerator for 24 hours or longer. Let stand at room temperature for 1 hour before serving. Serve with assorted party crackers or warm flour tortillas.

Merle Ellis, The Butcher

---

*Merle Ellis is author of **Cutting Up in the Kitchen**. This meat buying and trimming guide is an invaluable resource and full of great recipes.*

PICO DE GALLO

Yield: 25 servings

3 cups chopped onions
3 cups chopped firm tomatoes
2 (or 3) jalapeños, seeded, minced
3 tablespoons minced fresh cilantro

Juice of 2 limes
2 avocados, chopped
Garlic salt to taste
Salt and pepper to taste

Mix onions, tomatoes, jalapeños, cilantro, lime juice, avocados, garlic salt, salt and pepper together in glass bowl. Serve as dip with tortilla chips or as accompaniment to pork, beef, seafood or poultry. Best when prepared only a couple of hours before serving.

Jack Hofberger

SPICY SALSA

Yield: 20 servings

1 (20-ounce) can whole kernel corn, drained
1 (20-ounce) can black olives, drained, chopped
2 (4-ounce) cans chopped green chiles, drained
2 bunches of scallions, chopped

4 (or 5) slices pickled jalapeño, chopped
6 tablespoons fresh lime juice
3 tablespoons olive oil
Freshly ground pepper to taste

Combine corn, olives, green chiles, scallions, jalapeño, lime juice, olive oil and pepper in bowl; mix well. Marinate in refrigerator for 3 to 4 hours, stirring occasionally. Serve with blue, yellow or white corn chips. May add 1 teaspoon chopped fresh cilantro and sliced banana peppers to salsa.

Ardie Davis

HUMMUS

Yield: 8 servings

1	(16-ounce) can garbanzo beans, drained, rinsed	1	tablespoon chopped onion
½	cup olive oil	1	teaspoon salt
¼	cup lemon juice		Freshly ground pepper to taste
2	large cloves of garlic, minced	1	tablespoon chopped fresh parsley

Combine garbanzo beans and ¼ cup of the olive oil in food processor or blender container. Process until blended. Add remaining olive oil gradually, processing constantly until blended. Add lemon juice, garlic, onion, salt and pepper. Process until smooth. Stir in parsley. Spoon into ceramic serving bowl. Garnish with additional parsley. Serve with warm pita bread wedges and kalamata olives.

Gretchen Mueller

SAUSAGE CHEESE BALLS

Yield: 75 servings

1	pound sharp Cheddar cheese, chopped	1	pound hot sausage
		3½	cups baking mix

Heat cheese in saucepan over low heat until melted, stirring occasionally. Crumble sausage into cheese; mix well. Add baking mix; mix well. Shape by teaspoonfuls into balls; arrange on baking sheet. Freeze until firm. Store in sealable plastic bag in freezer until just before baking. Arrange frozen sausage cheese balls on baking sheet. Bake at 350° F for 15 to 20 minutes or until light brown.

John & Sue Beadle

John and Sue Beadle of the B.S. Cookers in Ada, Michigan, travel the country entering cooking contests. As Champion Chili Cooks, they have successfully broadened their horizons into barbeque competitions.

BUFFALO WINGS

Yield: 30 servings

3	pounds chicken wings, tips removed	1	teaspoon salt
1	cup vinegar	1	teaspoon pepper
1	tablespoon chili powder	1	(to 2) teaspoons red pepper sauce
1	tablespoon olive oil		
2	teaspoons Worcestershire sauce		

Rinse chicken and pat dry. Pour mixture of vinegar, chili powder, olive oil, Worcestershire sauce, salt, pepper and red pepper sauce over chicken in nonreactive dish, turning to coat. Marinate, covered, in refrigerator for 8 hours or longer, turning occasionally. Drain, reserving marinade. Grill over medium-hot coals for 30 to 40 minutes or until brown and crisp, turning and basting with reserved marinade frequently. Serve with bleu cheese dressing and celery sticks.

Donna McClure, P.D.T. (Pretty Damn Tasty)

Donna McClure, P.D.T., has twice won Grand Champion at the Tournament of Champions in Meridian, Texas. These Buffalo Wings are a spicy opener for Super Bowl Sunday at the McClure home.

'Que Tip

Marinate chicken in Italian salad dressing in the refrigerator for eight hours or longer for a great flavor.

NUCLEAR CHICKEN WINGS
Yield: 50 servings

5	pounds chicken wings, tips removed	1	tablespoon Cajun spice
1	cup barbeque spice	1	tablespoon cayenne
2	tablespoons crushed jalapeños	1	(to 2) cups spicy barbeque sauce

Rinse chicken and pat dry. Sprinkle mixture of barbeque spice, jalapeños, Cajun spice and cayenne over chicken in nonreactive dish, stirring to coat. Marinate, covered, in refrigerator for 8 hours or longer. Smoke chicken over indirect heat for 30 minutes, turning once. Baste both sides of wings with barbeque sauce. Grill over direct heat for 5 minutes per side. Serve immediately with your favorite spicy sauce.

Scott O'Meara

Scott O'Meara parlayed his love of barbeque from cooking in competition into his livelihood. He owns Boardroom BBQ in Overland Park, Kansas. This recipe won the 1990 Coors Buffalo Wings contest at the American Royal Barbecue Contest.

STUFFED MORELS
Yield: 30 servings

3	pounds fresh morels, cut into halves, rinsed	2	tablespoons minced onion
	Salt to taste	2	tablespoons minced celery
1	cup uncooked wild rice	1	teaspoon butter

Soak mushrooms in salt water to cover in bowl for 30 minutes; drain. Cook wild rice for 30 minutes using package directions. Sauté onion and celery in butter in skillet. Stir into wild rice. Arrange mushroom halves on sheet of heavy-duty foil. Top each half with 1 tablespoon of the rice mixture. Fold and seal foil tightly. Grill over hot coals for 10 minutes.

John Zellers

MARINATED MUSHROOMS

Yield: 12 servings

¾	cup vegetable oil	½	teaspoon salt
¼	cup red wine vinegar	¼	teaspoon ground pepper
1	teaspoon (heaping) thyme	¼	teaspoon rosemary
1	teaspoon (heaping) marjoram	2	(or 3) (4-ounce) cans button mushrooms, drained
2	cloves of garlic, sliced		

Combine first 8 ingredients in bowl; mix well. Add mushrooms, stirring gently to coat. Marinate, covered, in refrigerator for 8 hours or longer, stirring occasionally. Drain; spoon into serving bowl.

Donna McClure, P.D.T. (Pretty Damn Tasty)

Donna McClure, P.D.T., has won the "Best Lenexa Cooker" at the Great Lenexa Barbecue Battle more often than anyone else.

GRILLED OYSTERS

Yield: 36 servings

¾	cup olive oil	1	teaspoon freshly ground pepper
¼	cup balsamic vinegar		Salt to taste
¼	cup dry red wine		
2	cups fresh corn	4	slices bacon
6	basil leaves, finely minced	36	fresh oysters in shells, scrubbed
3	shallots, finely minced		

Whisk olive oil, balsamic vinegar and red wine together in bowl. Stir in corn, basil, shallots, pepper and salt. Let stand, covered, at room temperature for 1 hour or longer. Grill bacon over hot coals until brown and crisp; crumble. Grill oysters over hot coals until oyster shells pop open. Remove from grill; discard top shell. Place remaining oyster halves on serving platter. Top each oyster with 1 tablespoon of the corn mixture; sprinkle with bacon.

Beth Philion

SAUSAGE ROLLS

Yield: 6 servings

12 ounces pork sausage	1 cup shredded Colby
1 (10-count) can biscuits	cheese
2 tablespoons chopped	1 tablespoon brown sugar
onion	¼ teaspoon cinnamon
½ cup chopped apple	

Brown sausage in skillet, stirring until crumbly; drain. Cool. Place biscuits on floured pastry board; flatten and pinch seams together. Roll into 8x12-inch rectangle. Sprinkle sausage and remaining ingredients on rectangle. Roll to enclose filling; seal edge. Cut into 6 slices. Place slices in 2 greased disposable baking pans. Grill with lid down over medium-low indirect heat for 30 to 35 minutes or until rolls test done.

Marty Lynch, Gaelic Gourmets

Marty Lynch discovered the compatibility of great wine and barbeque about ten years ago. This, coupled with a good team and friendships he has developed through the years, demonstrated to him that this was his pot of gold at the end of the rainbow.

HOT BUTTERED RUM MIX

Yield: 100 servings

1 pound unsalted butter,	2 tablespoons whole cloves
softened	2 tablespoons cinnamon
2 cups packed brown sugar	2 tablespoons lemon juice
1 cup sugar	5 drops of maple extract

Combine all ingredients in bowl; mix well. Combine 1 teaspoon of butter mixture with 1 cup hot water and a shot of rum in mug for each serving. Garnish each serving with cinnamon stick. Store butter mixture in crock in refrigerator.

Jim "Trim" Tabb

Jim is founder of the North Carolina State Championship, the Blue Ridge Barbecue and Music Festival.

SIDE DISHES

~~

BEAN SALAD
Yield: 12 servings

1	(20-ounce) can red beans	2	tablespoons Dijon
1	(20-ounce) can green		mustard
	beans	2	teaspoons red wine
1	(20-ounce) can wax beans		vinegar
1	(20-ounce) can garbanzo	1	tablespoon lemon juice
	beans	1	teaspoon Louisiana hot
1	medium onion, chopped		sauce
3	tablespoons olive oil	1	clove of garlic, minced

Drain and rinse beans. Combine beans and onion in bowl; mix well. Pour mixture of olive oil, Dijon mustard, wine vinegar, lemon juice, hot sauce and garlic over bean mixture, stirring to coat. Chill, covered, for 2 to 8 hours before serving.

Rich & Bunny Tuttle, K-Cass Bar-B-Que

SOUTHWEST BEAN SALAD

Yield: 8 servings

1	(16-ounce) can black beans	½	cup chopped celery
1	(15-ounce) can kidney beans	1	tablespoon diced pimento
1	(15-ounce) can pinto beans	6	tablespoons olive oil
2	medium tomatoes, seeded, coarsely chopped	6	tablespoons salsa
		3	tablespoons red wine vinegar
1	cup sliced green onions with tops	½	teaspoon cumin
		1	cup sour cream

Drain and rinse beans twice. Combine beans, tomatoes, green onions, celery and pimento in bowl; mix gently. Pour mixture of olive oil, salsa, wine vinegar and cumin over bean mixture, stirring to coat. Chill, covered, for 8 hours or longer. Spoon onto lettuce-lined salad plates; top with sour cream.

Donna McClure, P.D.T. (Pretty Damn Tasty)

BROOKVILLE COLESLAW

Yield: 10 servings

1½	pounds green cabbage, chopped	⅔	cup sugar
		⅓	cup vinegar
1	teaspoon salt	1	cup whipping cream

Combine cabbage and salt in bowl; mix well. Chill, covered, for 3 hours. Add mixture of sugar, vinegar and whipping cream; mix well. Chill, covered, for 30 minutes or longer before serving.

Ivan "Sam" Houston, Salt City Sizzlers

MISSISSIPPI DELTA COLESLAW

Yield: 15 servings

1	large head green cabbage, shredded	2	green bell peppers, sliced into thin strips
2	medium onions, thinly sliced, separated into rings	1	cup sugar
		3/4	cup vegetable oil
		3/4	cup white vinegar

Place cabbage in large bowl. Layer onions and green peppers over cabbage; sprinkle with sugar. Drizzle with oil and vinegar. Chill, covered, for 2 to 8 hours. Toss just before serving.

Skip Gigliotti, Crispy Critters

Skip Gigliotti of the Crispy Critters is originally from Memphis. His team has members from seven states. They compete on both KCBS and Memphis in May circuits.

DILLED POTATO SALAD

Yield: 8 servings

1½	pounds small red potatoes, cooked, cut into quarters	1	tablespoon prepared mustard
2	tablespoons finely chopped fresh dillweed	½	teaspoon salt
		¼	teaspoon ground pepper
1	cup mayonnaise	½	cup sliced pimento-stuffed green olives
		⅓	cup sliced green onions

Combine red potatoes with mixture of dillweed, mayonnaise, mustard, salt and pepper in bowl; mix well. Stir in olives and green onions. Chill, covered, for 3 hours or longer before serving.

Janeyce Michel-Cupito, Powderpuff Barbeque

The Powderpuff Barbeque team, headed by Janeyce Michel-Cupito, was one of the first cooking teams led by a woman. Janeyce has been cooking in competition since 1984.

GERMAN POTATO SALAD
Yield: 12 servings

16 (to 24) small russet potatoes
1¼ cups olive oil
⅓ cup tarragon vinegar
1 tablespoon Dijon mustard

1 tablespoon snipped fresh dillweed or 1 teaspoon dried dillweed
½ teaspoon salt
¼ teaspoon freshly ground pepper

Peel a narrow strip around center of each potato. Combine potatoes with enough water to cover in saucepan. Cook for 20 to 25 minutes or until tender; drain. Cut into halves or into quarters. Place potatoes in large bowl. Combine olive oil, tarragon vinegar, Dijon mustard, dillweed, salt and pepper in food processor container fitted with steel blade. Process until blended. Pour over warm potatoes, turning to coat. Chill, covered, for 1 hour or longer. May add sieved hard-cooked eggs to potatoes before adding oil mixture.

Joan Matoole

Joan Matoole is heavily involved in the Greater Omaha BBQ Society. There is no recipe she can't unearth when the need arises. She is a valuable resource.

'Que Tip

Most fresh vegetables are ideal for grilling. Simply brush with olive or vegetable oil and grill just until tender.

OLD COUNTRY POTATO SALAD

Yield: 12 servings

6	medium potatoes, cooked, peeled, cubed	2	tablespoons Dijon mustard
5	hard-cooked eggs, chopped	1	tablespoon prepared yellow mustard
2	large dill pickles, chopped	1	teaspoon lemon juice
4	sweet pickles, chopped	1	teaspoon freshly ground pepper
1	medium yellow onion, chopped	1	teaspoon dillweed
½	cup sliced green olives	3	hard-cooked eggs, cut into wedges
1½	cups mayonnaise-type salad dressing		Paprika to taste

Combine potatoes, chopped eggs, dill pickles, sweet pickles, onion and olives in bowl; mix gently. Pour mixture of salad dressing, Dijon mustard, yellow mustard, lemon juice, pepper and dillweed over potato mixture, stirring to mix. Spoon into serving bowl. Garnish with egg wedges; sprinkle with paprika. Chill, covered, until serving time.

Ginger Stephens

Ginger Stephens won the first annual Yellow Daisy Great American Potato Salad Contest in Stone Mountain, Georgia, with this recipe.

'Que Tip

Any food that can be pan fried, broiled, or roasted indoors can be grilled or smoked.

TEXAS POTATO SALAD

Yield: 10 servings

1	large onion, chopped	1	teaspoon celery seeds
½	cup dill pickle juice	⅓	cup barbeque sauce
5	large baking potatoes	⅓	cup vinaigrette salad
	Salt to taste		dressing
	Pepper to taste	½	(to 1) cup mayonnaise

Marinate onion in pickle juice in bowl in refrigerator for 2 to 8 hours. Boil potatoes in salted water in saucepan until tender but slightly firm; drain. Cool in ice water in bowl; drain. Peel and chop potatoes. Place in bowl. Sprinkle with salt, pepper and celery seeds. Chill, covered, for 8 hours or longer. Drain onion, discarding pickle juice. Add onion to potato mixture; mix well. Stir in barbeque sauce and vinaigrette salad dressing. Chill, covered, for 1 hour or longer. Stir in mayonnaise just before serving. Adjust seasonings.

Great Chefs, Great BBQ

SAUERKRAUT SALAD

Yield: 6 servings

1	(16-ounce) can sauerkraut, drained	½	cup chopped celery
		¼	cup chopped pimentos
1	medium onion, finely chopped	1¼	cups sugar
		½	cup vegetable oil
½	cup chopped green bell pepper	½	cup white vinegar

Combine sauerkraut, onion, green pepper, celery and pimentos in bowl; mix well. Pour mixture of sugar, oil and vinegar over sauerkraut mixture, stirring to mix. Chill, covered, in refrigerator for 8 hours or longer before serving.

Sue Beadle, B.S. Cookers

CURRIED TURKEY & WILD RICE SALAD

Yield: 4 servings

½ cup wild rice, cooked
2 tablespoons vegetable oil
1 tablespoon vinegar
1 teaspoon salt
1 teaspoon curry powder
1 (10-ounce) package frozen green peas, cooked, cooled
2 cups chopped smoked turkey breast

1 cup chopped celery
¼ cup chopped green bell pepper
½ cup mayonnaise
3 cups mixed greens
1½ ounces slivered almonds, toasted

Combine wild rice with mixture of oil, vinegar, salt and curry powder in bowl; mix well. Chill, covered, for several hours. Add peas, turkey, celery and green pepper; mix well. Stir in mayonnaise. Spoon over mixed greens on serving platter; sprinkle with almonds.

Libby Hayes

'Que Tip

To grill small vegetables or vegetable pieces, thread onto water-soaked bamboo skewers for ease in turning.

GRILLED VEGETABLE GAZPACHO

Yield: 6 servings

1	red bell pepper, cut into halves, seeded	3	cloves of garlic
1	green bell pepper, cut into halves, seeded	2	slices dry bread
1	small red onion, cut into halves	5	tablespoons olive oil
½	small eggplant, cut into ½-inch slices	2	tablespoons balsamic vinegar
¼	cup olive oil	4	cups clamato juice
	Salt and pepper to taste	2	tablespoons chopped fresh basil
		¼	cup lemon juice

Rub bell peppers, red onion and eggplant with ¼ cup olive oil; sprinkle with salt and pepper. Grill peppers and onion over medium-hot coals for 2 to 3 minutes or until slightly charred, turning 1 or 2 times. Remove to platter; cut into thin slices. Grill eggplant slices over medium-hot coals for 2 to 3 minutes per side or until brown. Remove from heat. Let stand until cool. Chop. Purée garlic and bread in food processor. Add salt and pepper. Add 5 tablespoons olive oil gradually, processing constantly until blended. Add balsamic vinegar. Process for 15 seconds. Pour clamato juice into bowl; whisk in bread mixture. Stir in grilled vegetables gently. Chill, covered, for 2 to 4 hours. Stir in basil and lemon juice; adjust seasonings just before serving. Ladle into soup bowls. May store, covered, in refrigerator for up to 3 days.

Chris Schlesinger, **Thrill of the Grill**

Chris says "Barbeque taught me what I consider one of the cardinal principles of cooking: It's the cooking, not just the eating, that is to be enjoyed."

PHANTOM OF MEMPHIS GUMBO

Yield: 10 servings

2 cups chopped onions	³/₄ cup vegetable oil
1½ cups chopped green bell peppers	³/₄ cup flour
	1 tablespoon minced garlic
1 cup chopped celery	5½ (to 6) cups seafood stock
2 bay leaves	1 pound andouille sausage
2 teaspoons salt	or kielbasa sausage, cut
³/₄ teaspoon cayenne	into ½-inch pieces
½ teaspoon white pepper	1 pound peeled medium
½ teaspoon black pepper	shrimp
½ teaspoon thyme	1 pound crawfish
¼ teaspoon oregano	

Combine onions, green peppers and celery in bowl; mix well. Combine bay leaves, salt, cayenne, white pepper, black pepper, thyme and oregano in bowl; mix well. Heat oil in large skillet until hot. Add flour gradually, stirring constantly until blended. Cook for 2 to 4 minutes or until mixture turns medium to dark brown, stirring constantly. Stir in half the onion mixture. Cook for 1 to 2 minutes, stirring constantly. Add remaining onion mixture; mix well. Cook for 2 minutes longer. Stir in seasoning mixture. Cook for 1 to 2 minutes, stirring constantly. Add garlic. Cook for 1 minute, stirring constantly. Remove from heat. Bring stock to a boil in stockpot. Add vegetable mixture by spoonfuls, stirring well after each addition. Bring to a boil. Add sausage. Boil for 15 minutes, stirring occasionally; reduce heat. Simmer for 10 minutes, stirring occasionally. Add shrimp and crawfish; mix well. Bring to a boil. Cook until shrimp turn pink, stirring occasionally. Discard bay leaves. Ladle over hot cooked rice in soup bowls. Serve with crusty French bread. May substitute 12 ounces crab meat for crawfish.

Matt Fisher, Sideburns

SHRIMP & BARBEQUED SAUSAGE GUMBO
Yield: 8 servings

1	medium onion, chopped	¼	teaspoon rubbed sage
3	stalks celery, sliced	¼	teaspoon oregano
2	cloves of garlic, minced	¼	teaspoon dillweed
¼	cup butter	¼	teaspoon coriander
1	large Anaheim chile pepper, chopped	1	pound barbeque sausage links, smoked, sliced
1	green bell pepper, chopped	12	ounces medium shrimp, peeled
2	(16-ounce) cans chopped tomatoes	1	tablespoon Old Bay seasoning
1	(10-ounce) can beef broth	2	tablespoons olive oil
1	cup water	¼	cup flour
1	teaspoon freshly ground pepper	1	(20-ounce) can cut okra, drained

Sauté onion, celery and garlic in butter in stockpot for 5 minutes or just until vegetables are tender. Add chile pepper and green pepper. Sauté for 3 minutes. Stir in undrained tomatoes, broth, water, pepper, sage, oregano, dillweed and coriander. Simmer for 30 minutes, stirring occasionally. Sauté sausage, shrimp and Old Bay seasoning in hot olive oil in skillet until shrimp begin to turn opaque. Remove shrimp and sausage to platter, reserving pan drippings. Stir flour into pan drippings until blended. Cook over medium heat until of roux consistency, stirring constantly. Add to onion mixture in stockpot. Cook until thickened, stirring constantly. Add okra, sausage and shrimp. Simmer for 15 minutes, stirring occasionally. Ladle into soup bowls. May add ½ teaspoon MSG.

Matt Bilardo

---

*Matt Bilardo, of the Eisbilhildred Barbecue team, won the
Kansas State Championship—the Great Lenexa Barbecue Battle—
during the team's first time out in competition.*

COWPOKE BEANS

Yield: 8 servings

1	(2-pound) package dried pinto beans	2	(16-ounce) cans stewed tomatoes
8	slices bacon, chopped	3	tablespoons plus 1 teaspoon chili powder
2	cloves of garlic, minced	1	teaspoon cumin
2	teaspoons salt	1	teaspoon marjoram
1	teaspoon crushed red pepper		Salt to taste
3	cups chopped onions		

Sort and rinse beans. Soak beans in enough water to cover in bowl for 8 hours or longer; drain. Combine beans with enough water to cover in saucepan. Stir in bacon, garlic, salt and red pepper. Cook, covered, for 1 1/2 hours or until beans are tender. Sauté onions in nonstick skillet. Add undrained tomatoes, chili powder, cumin, marjoram and salt; mix well. Simmer for 45 minutes, stirring occasionally. Add to bean mixture; mix well. Simmer for 20 minutes longer, stirring occasionally.

Tom Wallace, Lone Wolf Cookers

Tom Wallace of the Lone Wolf Cookers is a previous Grand Champion of the American Royal Open Barbecue Contest.

'Que Tip

Place baked beans or other vegetables in your smoker to get a smoked flavor. Do not oversmoke; the beans or vegetables should be partially cooked before smoking.

SLOW-COOKER BAKED BEANS

Yield: 12 servings

1	pound bacon, chopped	1	(16-ounce) can jalapeño
1	onion, chopped		pinto beans
1	(16-ounce) can lima	½	cup packed brown sugar
	beans, drained	½	cup catsup
1	(16-ounce) can red	1	tablespoon
	kidney beans, drained		Worcestershire sauce
1	(16-ounce) can Great	1	tablespoon vinegar
	Northern white beans,		
	drained		

Sauté bacon and onion in skillet. Combine bacon mixture with lima beans, red kidney beans, white beans, undrained jalapeño pinto beans, brown sugar, catsup, Worcestershire sauce and vinegar in slow cooker; mix well. Cook on Low for 6 hours, stirring occasionally.

Pam Buck

Pam Buck is the chairperson for the Blue Springs Barbeque Blaze-Off.
She runs a well-organized event.

'Que Tip

Do not use cedar, fir, pine, spruce, or eucalyptus
wood; their smoke gives meat a bitter flavor.

GLAZED CARROTS

Yield: 6 servings

6 medium carrots, cut into ¼-inch thick slices	2 tablespoons confectioners' sugar
2 tablespoons butter or margarine	⅛ teaspoon salt
¼ teaspoon lemon zest	Pepper to taste

Place carrot slices in center of large sheet of heavy-duty foil. Dot carrots with butter and sprinkle with lemon zest. Fold and seal foil tightly. Grill foil package over hot coals for 25 to 30 minutes or until carrots are tender. Spoon carrots into serving bowl; sprinkle with confectioners' sugar, salt and pepper.

Jim & Debbie Wilmes, Summer 'N Smoke

CORN CASSEROLE

Yield: 8 servings

3 ears of corn	2 eggs, slightly beaten
½ cup butter	½ teaspoon freshly ground pepper
1 (17-ounce) can cream-style corn	½ teaspoon salt
1 (9-ounce) package corn bread mix	1 cup sour cream
1 (4-ounce) can chopped green chiles	1 cup shredded sharp Cheddar cheese

Remove kernels of corn with sharp knife into bowl; scrape corncob with knife to remove juice. Heat butter in 9x13-inch aluminum pan over hot coals until melted. Stir in fresh corn kernels, cream-style corn, corn bread mix, green chiles, eggs, pepper and salt. Drop sour cream by spoonfuls evenly over mixture; fold in gently. Sprinkle with cheese. Place pan on grill rack. Bake, covered with foil, over hot coals for 1 hour or until set. May bake in 350° F oven for 35 to 40 minutes or until set.

Janeyce Michel-Cupito, Powderpuff Barbeque

PARSLIED CORN IN THE HUSK

Yield: 8 servings

8 ears of unhusked corn	¼ cup minced fresh chives
½ cup butter or margarine, softened	¼ teaspoon garlic powder
	Salt and pepper to taste
¼ cup chopped fresh parsley	

Pull corn husks back, leaving husks attached at base of cob; remove silk. Soak corn in enough water to cover in large bowl for 20 minutes; drain. Brush corn kernels with mixture of butter, parsley, chives, garlic powder, salt and pepper. Reposition husks. Wrap corn in foil; twist ends. Arrange corn on grill rack in covered grill. Cook with lid down over medium-hot coals for 30 minutes. Remove foil and pull husks down; tie husks at base of cob to form handle. May bake in 400° F oven for 25 minutes.

Ron Fisher, Sideburns

TEX-MEX BARBEQUED CORN

Yield: 6 servings

6 ears of unhusked corn	1 teaspoon kosher salt
⅓ cup butter	Chili powder to taste
Lime juice to taste	

Do not trim, open or remove silk. Soak corn in cool water in bowl for 30 minutes if husks are dry. Grill over hot coals until tender, turning frequently. Pull husks back; tie husks at base to form handle. Brush corn with butter; drizzle with lime juice. Sprinkle with salt and chili powder. May bake in 400° F oven for 20 minutes.

Ralph Blevins, Rutherford's Ol' South

MUSHROOM CASSEROLE

Yield: 8 servings

8	slices white bread	³/₄	teaspoon salt
¹/₂	cup butter	¹/₄	teaspoon pepper
1	pound fresh mushrooms, sliced	1¹/₂	cups milk
¹/₂	cup chopped onion	2	eggs, slightly beaten
¹/₂	cup chopped celery	1	(10-ounce) can cream of mushroom soup
¹/₂	cup chopped green bell pepper	¹/₂	cup shredded Cheddar cheese
¹/₂	cup mayonnaise		

Spread bread on both sides with 4 tablespoons of the butter. Cut 3 slices of the bread into 1-inch cubes, reserving remaining bread. Arrange bread cubes in buttered baking dish; set aside. Sauté mushrooms in 2 tablespoons of the butter in skillet until most of liquid has evaporated. Spread mushrooms over bread cubes. Sauté onion, celery and green pepper in remaining 2 tablespoons butter in skillet until vegetables are tender. Stir in mayonnaise, salt and pepper. Spread over prepared layers. Cut 3 slices of the reserved bread into 1-inch cubes; sprinkle over vegetable mixture. Pour mixture of milk and eggs over prepared layers. Chill for 1 hour or longer. Spread with soup. Cut remaining 2 slices of reserved bread into 1-inch cubes; sprinkle over top. Bake at 350° F for 40 to 50 minutes or until brown and bubbly. Sprinkle with cheese. Bake for 10 minutes longer.

Donna McClure, P.D.T. (Pretty Damn Tasty)

'Que Tip

To prevent fresh mushrooms from becoming soft, clean by
wiping with a damp cloth rather than soaking in water.

BARBEQUED VIDALIA ONIONS

Yield: 8 servings

1	(to 2) teaspoons olive oil
4	Vidalia onions, cut into quarters
1	(12-ounce) can beer

Salt and freshly ground pepper to taste
½ cup butter
Cayenne to taste

Grease bottom of round aluminum pan with olive oil. Arrange onions in pan. Add enough beer to cover onions by ½ inch. Sprinkle onions with salt and pepper. Top each onion quarter with pat of butter; sprinkle with cayenne. Place pan on grill rack. Grill, covered with foil, over medium-hot coals for 45 minutes or until onions are tender.

Terry Emo

PICKLED ONIONS

Yield: 12 servings

½ cup olive oil
2 pounds white onions, cut into ⅛-inch wedges
1½ cups sugar
1 cup red wine vinegar
¼ cup catsup

2 tablespoons sea salt
2 teaspoons red pepper flakes
Freshly ground white pepper to taste

Heat olive oil in heavy saucepan over low heat. Stir in onions. Cook, covered, for 15 minutes or until tender, stirring occasionally. Add sugar, wine vinegar, catsup, sea salt, red pepper flakes and white pepper; mix well. Simmer for 3 minutes, stirring occasionally. Serve warm or at room temperature. May be prepared up to 5 days in advance and stored, covered, in refrigerator until day of serving.

Jim Trimble

Jim Trimble is an environmental attorney as well as a foodie.

PEAS & GARLIC

Yield: 10 servings

¼ cup olive oil	2 tablespoons tomato paste
3 tablespoons flour	2 pounds frozen peas, thawed
3 medium onions, chopped	½ cup (or more) hot water
8 large cloves of garlic, minced	1 tablespoon pepper
1 bunch of parsley, minced	

Combine olive oil and flour in saucepan; mix well. Cook over medium heat until dark brown, stirring constantly; reduce heat. Stir in onions. Sauté until tender. Add garlic and parsley; mix well. Sauté for 10 minutes longer. Stir in tomato paste and peas, stirring well after each addition. Add hot water ½ cup at a time until sauce just coats peas. Stir in pepper. Simmer for 20 minutes, stirring frequently.

David Veljacic, Sum Young Guy

GARLIC NEW POTATOES

Yield: 8 servings

8 whole uncooked new potatoes	½ (to 1) teaspoon kosher salt
½ cup garlic oil	½ (to 1) teaspoon freshly ground pepper

Brush potatoes with some of garlic oil; sprinkle with salt and pepper. Grill over hot coals for 45 minutes or until tender, turning and basting with remaining garlic oil frequently. May stir ground dried chiles, chili powder, minced fresh dillweed or other fresh herbs into garlic oil. Grill large, whole partially cooked potatoes for 15 to 20 minutes, ½-inch uncooked potato wedges for 8 to 10 minutes and ¼-inch uncooked potato slices for 6 to 8 minutes.

*Leslie Beal Bloom, **Barbecue Sizzling Fireside Know-How***

GRILLED CHEESE POTATOES

Yield: 4 servings

1   (to 2) teaspoons vegetable oil

8   unpeeled red potatoes, cut into cubes

1   large red onion, finely chopped

½   cup butter, chopped

½   cup shredded Swiss cheese

¼   cup grated Parmesan cheese

½   teaspoon garlic powder
    Salt and pepper to taste

Brush large sheet heavy-duty foil with oil. Place potatoes and onion in center of foil. Add butter, Swiss cheese, Parmesan cheese, garlic powder, salt and pepper; mix gently. Fold and seal foil; double wrap with heavy-duty foil. Grill over hot coals for 25 minutes per side.

Darrell & Karen DeGreve, Bearly Smokin'

TWICE-BAKED POTATOES ON THE GRILL

Yield: 6 servings

6   large baking potatoes

½   cup half-and-half

½   cup shredded Gruyère cheese

Chopped fresh chives to taste

Paprika to taste

Wrap potatoes in foil. Place on and around hot coals in grill. Cook for 40 minutes. Remove potatoes; discard foil. Cut small slit from top of each potato. Scoop out pulp, leaving shells intact. Combine potato pulp, half-and-half and cheese in bowl; mix well. Spoon into reserved shells; sprinkle with chives and paprika. Wrap each potato loosely with foil. Place on grill rack. Grill over hot coals for 15 minutes. May substitute grated Parmesan cheese for Gruyère cheese.

Rich & Bunny Tuttle, K-Cass Bar-B-Que

FRIED SWEET POTATOES

Yield: 8 servings

4 medium sweet potatoes,
peeled, cut lengthwise
into ¼-inch strips

4 cups peanut oil
Salt to taste
Cayenne to taste

Soak sweet potatoes in ice water in bowl for 15 minutes; drain on paper towels. Deep-fry in peanut oil heated to 375° F to 400° F in skillet until sweet potato strips begin to float to top or turn over. Drain on paper towels; sprinkle lightly with salt and cayenne.

Bob Zaban, Mr. Z's

GRILLED SWEET POTATOES WITH MOLASSES GLAZE

Yield: 8 servings

4 medium sweet potatoes
Salt to taste
¼ cup molasses
Juice of ½ orange
1 tablespoon unsalted
butter, softened

⅛ teaspoon allspice
Salt and freshly cracked
pepper to taste

Peel sweet potatoes; cut lengthwise into ½-inch slices. Combine sweet potatoes and salt with enough water to cover in saucepan. Cook for 8 to 10 minutes or just until tender but firm; drain. Cool to room temperature. Combine molasses, orange juice, butter, allspice, salt and pepper in bowl; mix well. Grill sweet potato slices over medium-hot coals for 2 to 3 minutes per side or until light brown. Brush both sides with molasses mixture. Grill for 30 seconds per side or just until glazed.

*Chris Schlesinger, **Thrill of the Grill***

Chris Schlesinger operates Jake & Earls Barbecue in Cambridge, Massachusetts.

SWEET POTATO CASSEROLE

Yield: 6 servings

3	cups mashed cooked sweet potatoes	1	teaspoon vanilla extract
½	cup melted butter	½	cup packed brown sugar
⅓	cup milk	¼	cup flour
¼	cup packed brown sugar	½	teaspoon allspice
2	eggs, beaten	½	cup chopped pecans
		2½	tablespoons melted butter

Combine sweet potatoes, ½ cup butter, milk, ¼ cup brown sugar, eggs and vanilla in bowl; mix well. Spoon into buttered baking dish. Combine ½ cup brown sugar, flour and allspice in bowl; mix well. Stir in pecans. Sprinkle over prepared layer; drizzle with 2½ tablespoons butter. Bake at 350° F for 25 minutes.

Donna McClure, P.D.T. (Pretty Damn Tasty)

GRILLED VEGETABLES

Yield: 10 servings

2	large Vidalia onions, thinly sliced		Salt and white pepper to taste
2	large baking potatoes, thinly sliced	2	tablespoons water
3	(or 4) large yellow squash, thinly sliced		Chopped fresh chives to taste
6	tablespoons butter or margarine		

Arrange onions, potatoes and yellow squash on large sheet of heavy-duty foil; dot with butter. Sprinkle with salt and white pepper; drizzle with water. Top with chives. Fold and seal foil tightly; pierce foil several times with fork. Grill over hot coals for 30 minutes or until vegetables are tender.

Steve & Melody Morgan, Vienna Volunteer Fire Department Cooking Team

MARGARITAVILLE VEGGIES
Yield: 8 servings

2 tomatoes, cut into quarters	¼ cup vegetable oil
4 small yellow squash, cut into halves	3 tablespoons tequila
	1½ tablespoons Triple Sec
1 medium zucchini, cut diagonally into 2-inch slices	2 tablespoons kosher salt
	2 tablespoons chili powder
8 green onions, cut into 3-inch pieces	Juice of 2 limes

Combine tomatoes, yellow squash, zucchini and green onions in bowl; mix well. Pour mixture of oil, tequila, Triple Sec, kosher salt and chili powder over vegetables, stirring to coat. Grill vegetables over hot coals until vegetables are tender, turning frequently. Remove to platter; drizzle with lime juice. Garnish with lime wedges, fresh cilantro and sliced jalapeños.

"Chef Dan" Morey, Team K.C.

"Chef Dan" Morey produces a line of barbeque sauces. He uses
fresh ingredients and turbinado sugar in his sauces.

'Que Tip

Foods wrapped in foil and cooked on a grill
should be turned frequently to prevent burning
and ensure even cooking.

STIR-FRY VEGETABLES
Yield: 8 servings

Florets of ½ bunch
broccoli
Florets of ½ head
cauliflower
½ green bell pepper, cut
into strips
½ yellow bell pepper, cut
into strips
½ red bell pepper, cut into
strips

1 small zucchini, sliced
1 small onion, sliced
½ cup snow peas
½ cup soy sauce
1 tablespoon sherry
1 teaspoon lemon zest
1 teaspoon lemon juice
1 teaspoon Greek seasoning
3 cloves of garlic, minced

Combine broccoli, cauliflower, green pepper, yellow pepper, red pepper, zucchini, onion and snow peas in sealable plastic bag. Pour mixture of soy sauce, sherry, lemon zest, lemon juice, Greek seasoning and garlic over vegetable mixture; seal tightly. Marinate at room temperature for 10 to 20 minutes, turning occasionally. Pour mixture into grill-top wok; place on grill rack. Cook at 250° F for 20 minutes or until done to taste, turning vegetables every 5 to 7 minutes.

Mick Harrison, **Hasty-Bake: The Simple Seven-Day Grill Book**

'Que Tip
Commercial salad dressings make delicious
marinades for vegetables.

DEVILED EGGS

Yield: 12 servings

6 hard-cooked eggs, cut into halves	½ teaspoon curry powder
¼ cup mayonnaise	¼ teaspoon salt
1 tablespoon sweet pickle relish	¼ teaspoon dry mustard
1 teaspoon vinegar	⅛ teaspoon freshly ground pepper
½ teaspoon Worcestershire sauce	⅛ teaspoon sugar
	⅛ teaspoon Tabasco sauce
	Paprika to taste

Remove yolks carefully from eggs, reserving whites. Combine egg yolks, mayonnaise, pickle relish, vinegar, Worcestershire sauce, curry powder, salt, dry mustard, pepper, sugar and Tabasco sauce in bowl, stirring with fork until mixed. Spoon egg yolk mixture into white halves; sprinkle with paprika. Arrange on serving platter. Chill, covered, until serving time. May thicken egg yolk mixture with instant potatoes or fine dry bread crumbs.

Jim "Trim" Tabb

Jim "Trim" Tabb spreads the gospel of 'Que in his travels around the world. He is a Ph.B., Doctor of Barbeque Philosophy, and a KCBS Certified Barbeque Judge.

'Que Tip

Prepare roasted red peppers by rubbing all sides of red peppers with vegetable oil. Grill over hot coals until blistered and charred on all sides, turning frequently. Place the red peppers in a sealable plastic bag; seal tightly. Let stand until the red peppers are cool and skins can be easily removed.

GRITS SOUFFLE

Yield: 6 servings

2¼ cups milk
½ cup uncooked grits
1   teaspoon salt
½ cup butter
4   egg yolks, beaten

¼ cup grated Parmesan
    cheese
6   egg whites
½ teaspoon cream of tartar

Heat milk in saucepan. Stir in grits and salt. Cook over low heat for 16 minutes, stirring constantly. Remove from heat. Add butter, stirring until melted. Stir a small amount of hot mixture into egg yolks; stir egg yolks into hot mixture. Add cheese; mix well. Cool for 10 minutes. Beat egg whites in mixer bowl until foamy; add cream of tartar. Beat until stiff peaks form. Beat ¼ of the egg whites into grits mixture. Fold in remaining egg whites. Spoon into soufflé dish. Bake at 350° F for 30 to 40 minutes; do not overcook.

Sally Uhl

Sally and Alan Uhl, of the Buffalo Chips-Dung Ho team of Lenexa, Kansas, are former Kansas State Barbecue Champions. The year following their win, their son Vic earned that same title.

'Que Tip

The expression "go whole hog" originated in the 18th century when the English shilling was called a "hog." Thus, a spendthrift, one willing to spend an entire shilling on the entertainment of a friend in a pub, was willing to "go whole hog."

KICKIN' HOPPIN' JOHN

Yield: 6 servings

1 pound dried black-eyed peas	1 teaspoon red pepper flakes
6 cups water	1 clove of garlic, minced
1 salt-cured ham hock	½ teaspoon freshly ground black pepper
1 medium onion, chopped	1 bay leaf

Sort and rinse peas. Bring peas and water to a boil in stockpot. Boil for 2 minutes. Remove from heat. Let stand for 1 hour. Stir in ham hock, onion and seasonings. Bring to a boil; reduce heat. Simmer, covered, for 2 hours, stirring occasionally; remove cover. Simmer until thickened, stirring occasionally. Discard ham hock and bay leaf.

Rich & Bunny Tuttle, K-Cass Bar-B-Que

SKILLET HOPPING JOHN

Yield: 6 servings

1 large onion, chopped	2 cups chicken or vegetable bouillon
2 large cloves of garlic, crushed	1 teaspoon salt
2 tablespoons melted butter or margarine	½ teaspoon crushed red pepper
2 (16-ounce) cans black-eyed peas, drained, rinsed	1 cup uncooked long grain rice

Sauté onion and garlic in butter in saucepan until tender. Stir in black-eyed peas, bouillon, salt, red pepper and rice. Bring to a boil; reduce heat. Simmer, covered, for 20 minutes or until liquid has evaporated and rice is tender. Serve with additional crushed red pepper.

Tom Wallace, Lone Wolf Cookers

MEXICAN RICE CASSEROLE

Yield: 8 servings

3 cups uncooked instant rice

1 (15-ounce) can Mexican stewed tomatoes

1 (10-ounce) can cream of chicken soup

1 (10-ounce) can cream of mushroom soup

1 (4-ounce) can diced green chiles

½ cup chopped green onions

½ cup chopped red onion

Combine rice, undrained tomatoes, soups, green chiles, green onions and red onion in bowl; mix well. Spoon into buttered 2-quart microwave-safe dish. Microwave for 12 to 15 minutes or until vegetables and rice are tender.

Patricia Coryell, Mrs. BBQ

---

*Patricia Coryell, of the Tacoma Aroma barbeque team,
is a former Oregon State Champion.*

WILDER THAN WILD RICE

Yield: 6 servings

¾ cup chopped onion

½ green bell pepper, chopped

½ red bell pepper, chopped

2 cloves of garlic, minced

1 tablespoon olive oil

1½ cups white rice

½ cup wild rice

1 (16-ounce) can black beans, drained

2½ cups water

Sauté onion, green pepper, red pepper and garlic in olive oil in saucepan until vegetables are tender. Stir in white rice and wild rice. Sauté for 1 minute. Add black beans and water; mix well. Cook over low heat for 40 minutes, stirring occasionally. Spoon into baking pan. Grill over hot coals for 5 minutes to add smoky flavor.

Mick Harrison, **Hasty-Bake: The Simple Seven-Day Grill Book**

ROSEMARY APPLE SALSA

Yield: 18 servings

¾ cup chopped yellow bell pepper

¾ cup chopped Granny Smith apple

¾ cup chopped Braeburn or Jonathan apple

¼ cup chopped dried apricots

3 tablespoons minced green onions

3 tablespoons lemon juice

1½ tablespoons extra-virgin olive oil

1 tablespoon finely chopped fresh rosemary

½ teaspoon salt

Freshly ground pepper to taste

Combine yellow pepper, apples, apricots, green onions, lemon juice, olive oil, rosemary, salt and pepper in bowl; mix well. Chill, covered, for 1 hour before serving.

Karen Adler

Karen Adler served this dish for a media event at Tavern on the Green in New York City. The food writers loved it!

BEER & CHEESE BREAD

Yield: 12 servings

3 cups self-rising flour

1 cup shredded Cheddar cheese

3 tablespoons sugar

1 teaspoon poppy seeds

½ teaspoon dry mustard

¼ teaspoon dillweed

1 (12-ounce) can flat beer, at room temperature

¼ cup melted butter

Combine flour, cheese, sugar, poppy seeds, dry mustard and dillweed in bowl; mix well. Stir in beer. Spoon into greased loaf pan. Let stand for 15 minutes. Bake at 325° F for 45 minutes. Drizzle butter over top. Bake for 15 minutes longer or until golden brown. Serve warm. May add ½ teaspoon garlic powder.

Omer "Mike" Nelson

BACON & CHILI CORN BREAD

Yield: 10 servings

3	slices bacon, chopped	1	egg
3	tablespoons chopped onion	1	cup milk
1	cup yellow cornmeal	1	(9-ounce) can whole kernel corn, drained
1	cup flour	1	(4-ounce) can chopped green chiles
1	tablespoon baking powder		
1	teaspoon salt		

Fry bacon in cast-iron skillet until crisp. Add onion. Cook until onion is tender, stirring frequently. Combine cornmeal, flour, baking powder and salt in bowl; mix well. Stir in mixture of egg and milk. Add corn and green chiles; mix well. Fold in undrained bacon and onion mixture. Heat same skillet in 425° F oven until hot. Pour corn bread mixture into skillet. Bake for 20 minutes. Serve with butter. May heat skillet over hot coals.

Merle Ellis, The Butcher

BROCCOLI & CHEESE CORN BREAD

Yield: 16 servings

1	small onion, chopped	1	(10-ounce) package frozen chopped broccoli, cooked
1	cup melted butter	1	cup cottage cheese
2	(9-ounce) packages corn bread mix	3	cups shredded Cheddar cheese
4	eggs, beaten		

Sauté onion in butter in skillet. Let stand until cool. Combine undrained onion with corn bread mix, eggs, broccoli, cottage cheese and 2 cups of the Cheddar cheese in bowl; mix well. Spoon into large greased cast-iron skillet or greased 9x13-inch baking pan. Sprinkle with remaining cheese. Bake at 400° F for 30 minutes. Serve hot.

Jo Ann Horton, Goat Gap Gazette

DESSERTS

～～

GRILLED STUFFED APPLES
Yield: 4 servings

4	large baking apples	2	tablespoons chopped
½	cup raisins		maraschino cherries
½	cup dry sherry	⅛	teaspoon cinnamon
2	tablespoons chopped	⅛	teaspoon ground cloves
	walnuts	⅛	teaspoon nutmeg
2	tablespoons brown sugar	1	tablespoon butter

Core apples, enlarging hole slightly. Place each apple on 12x18-inch sheet of heavy-duty foil. Spoon mixture of raisins, sherry, walnuts, brown sugar, cherries, cinnamon, cloves and nutmeg into apples; dot with butter. Fold and seal foil loosely. Grill over low heat for 1 hour or until apples are done to taste. Serve with vanilla ice cream. May substitute water for sherry.

J. L. (Mad Marty) Patty

BARBEQUED BANANAS

Yield: 10 servings

10 bananas	Allspice to taste
Lemon juice to taste	½ cup butter
1 cup packed brown sugar	
Cinnamon or nutmeg to taste	

Place each banana on sheet of heavy-duty foil. Brush with lemon juice; sprinkle with brown sugar. Dust lightly with cinnamon and allspice; dot with butter. Fold and seal foil; twist ends. Grill over hot coals for 10 minutes, turning occasionally.

Clayton Zellers, Smokes Up

'Que Tip

The open lands of the West encouraged large-scale hog raising operations which, in turn, created a need for expanded commercial pork processing facilities. Packing plants grew throughout the Midwest, with centrally located Cincinnati soon becoming so strongly associated with pork production that it became known, informally at least, as "Porkopolis."

DIVINE CHEESECAKE

Yield: 12 servings

1	(to 2) teaspoons vegetable oil	2	teaspoons grated lemon rind
1	cup graham cracker crumbs	5	eggs
3	tablespoons sugar	1	cup sugar
¼	teaspoon cinnamon	¼	teaspoon salt
3	tablespoons melted butter	1½	cups sour cream
24	ounces cream cheese, softened	2	tablespoons sugar
		½	teaspoon vanilla extract
		1	(21-ounce) can cherry pie filling

Grease bottom and sides of 9-inch springform pan lightly with oil. Combine graham cracker crumbs, 3 tablespoons sugar and cinnamon in bowl; mix well. Stir in butter. Press evenly over bottom and 2 inches up side of prepared pan. Chill in refrigerator. Beat cream cheese and lemon rind in mixer bowl until blended. Add eggs, 1 cup sugar and salt. Beat for 10 minutes or until smooth, scraping bowl occasionally. Spoon over chilled layer. Bake at 350° F for 50 minutes or until set. Cool on wire rack for 20 minutes; cheesecake will crack during cooling process. Beat sour cream, 2 tablespoons sugar and vanilla in mixer bowl until smooth. Spread evenly over baked layer. Bake for 10 to 12 minutes longer or until set. Cool on wire rack. Chill in refrigerator. Place cheesecake on serving plate; remove side of pan. Spread top with pie filling. Chill until serving time. May store in refrigerator for up to 2 days.

Bill Robinson, Fire N' Smoke

'Que Tip

Chips of hickory, mesquite, or other woods may be soaked in water and added to the hot coals to impart various flavors to foods.

SAUSALITO'S CHEESECAKE
Yield: 18 servings

1½ cups graham cracker crumbs
½ cup melted unsalted butter
1 cup finely chopped pecans
24 ounces cream cheese, softened
4 eggs
3½ cups cane sugar
1 tablespoon lemon juice
3 cups sour cream
½ cup cane sugar
1 tablespoon lemon juice

Combine graham cracker crumbs and butter in bowl; mix well. Stir in pecans. Press into 10x14-inch baking pan. Beat cream cheese, eggs, 3½ cups sugar and 1 tablespoon lemon juice in mixer bowl until creamy. Spoon over prepared layer. Place on middle oven rack. Bake at 350° F until set. Beat sour cream, ½ cup sugar and 1 tablespoon lemon juice in mixer bowl for 5 minutes, scraping bowl occasionally. Spread over baked layers. Let stand for 20 minutes. Chill in refrigerator.

JoAnn Horton, **Goat Gap Gazette**

JoAnn Horton, editor of the **Goat Gap Gazette**, *is a free-lance food writer in the Houston area. She is a legend in the chili world.*

'Que Tip

The phrase "pork barrel politics" is derived from the pre-Civil War practice of distributing salt pork to the slaves from huge barrels. By the 1870s, congressmen were referring to regularly dipping into the "pork barrel" to obtain funds for popular projects in their home districts.

GOOEY BUTTER DESSERT

Yield: 15 servings

1 (2-layer) package yellow cake mix	2 eggs, beaten
2 eggs, beaten	1 (1-pound) package confectioners' sugar
½ cup melted butter	¼ cup confectioners' sugar
8 ounces cream cheese, softened	

Combine cake mix, eggs and butter in bowl; mix well. Pat into greased 9x13-inch baking pan. Beat cream cheese, eggs and 1 pound confectioners' sugar in mixer bowl until smooth. Spread over prepared layer; sprinkle with ¼ cup confectioners' sugar. Bake at 350° F for 40 to 45 minutes or until edges are brown and pull from sides of pan. Let stand until cool. Cut into squares.

Donna McClure, P.D.T. (Pretty Damn Tasty)

HOMEMADE VANILLA ICE CREAM

Yield: 12 servings

2 cups milk	2 cups half-and-half
1¾ cups sugar	1 tablespoon vanilla extract
½ teaspoon salt	4 cups whipping cream

Scald milk in saucepan until bubbles form around edges of pan. Remove from heat. Add sugar and salt, stirring until dissolved. Stir in half-and-half, vanilla and whipping cream. Chill, covered, for 30 minutes. Pour into ice cream freezer container. Freeze using manufacturer's directions.

Frank & Judy Bronson, Bar-Be-Que 2

'Que Tip
Use a water-filled spray bottle to extinguish flare-ups.

STRAWBERRY SHORTCAKE ROYALE

Yield: 12 servings

1	cup vanilla ice cream, softened	4	cups strawberries, cut into halves
½	cup sour cream	⅓	cup shortening
¼	cup sugar	2½	cups buttermilk baking mix
1	teaspoon vanilla extract		
1	cup whipping cream, whipped	¾	cup milk
		3	tablespoons sugar
⅓	cup sugar	1	teaspoon vanilla extract

Combine ice cream, sour cream, ¼ cup sugar and 1 teaspoon vanilla in bowl; mix well. Fold in whipped cream. Chill, covered, in refrigerator. Sprinkle ⅓ cup sugar over strawberries in bowl. Let stand for 30 minutes. Cut shortening into baking mix in bowl until crumbly. Stir in mixture of milk, 3 tablespoons sugar and 1 teaspoon vanilla. Pat into 2 greased 8-inch round baking pans. Bake at 425° F for 12 to 15 minutes or until golden brown. Remove to wire rack to cool. Place 1 baked layer on serving plate; top with strawberries. Place remaining baked layer over the strawberries. Spread ice cream mixture evenly over top and side of shortcake. Chill until serving time.

Libby Hayes

'Que Tip

Coat a clean grill rack with olive oil or spray with
nonstick cooking spray before using.

FROSTED BROWNIES

Yield: 36 servings

1 cup sugar	6 tablespoons butter
½ cup butter, softened	6 tablespoons milk
4 eggs	1⅓ cups sugar
1 (16-ounce) can chocolate syrup	1 cup chocolate chips
1 cup plus 1 tablespoon flour	

Beat 1 cup sugar, ½ cup butter and eggs in mixer bowl until smooth. Add chocolate syrup and flour; mix well. Spoon into greased 11x15-inch baking pan. Bake at 350° F for 20 minutes. Bring 6 tablespoons butter, milk and 1⅓ cups sugar to a boil in saucepan; reduce heat. Simmer for 1 minute, stirring constantly. Remove from heat. Add chocolate chips, beating until smooth. Spread over baked layer. Let stand until cool. Cut into squares.

Karen Peterson & Harold Jansen, Tap & Trawf Kookers

Karen Peterson, of the Tap & Trawf Kookers of Overland Park, Kansas, earned a first place award from the Pee Wee Judges at Gladstone, Missouri, and Lenexa, Kansas, with this recipe.

'Que Tip

Use water in your smoker to form steam to help retain moisture in meat. Place water pan directly under meat so the meat can be self-basting.

LEMON BARS

Yield: 36 servings

2	cups flour	¼	cup flour
½	cup confectioners' sugar	1	teaspoon baking powder
1	cup butter	4	eggs, beaten
2	cups sugar	6	tablespoons lemon juice

Combine 2 cups flour and confectioners' sugar in bowl; mix well. Cut in butter until crumbly. Press into lightly greased 9x13-inch baking pan. Bake at 350° F for 15 minutes. Combine sugar, ¼ cup flour and baking powder in bowl; mix well. Stir in eggs and lemon juice. Spread over baked layer. Bake for 25 minutes longer. Cool. Sprinkle with additional confectioners' sugar; cut into bars.

John & Sue Beadle, B.S. Cookers

Sue serves these quick-and-easy lemon bars to cleanse barbeque-saturated palates, as well as to provide the perfect ending to any meal.

WHITE CHOCOLATE MACADAMIA COOKIES

Yield: 36 servings

¾	cup packed brown sugar	1	teaspoon baking soda
½	cup sugar	½	teaspoon salt
1	cup butter, softened	8	ounces white chocolate, coarsely chopped
1	egg		
2	teaspoons vanilla extract	3½	ounces macadamia nuts, coarsely chopped
1¾	cups flour		

Beat brown sugar, sugar and butter in mixer bowl until light and fluffy. Add egg and vanilla; mix well. Stir in flour, baking soda and salt. Add white chocolate and macadamia nuts; mix well. Drop by rounded tablespoonfuls 3 inches apart onto ungreased cookie sheet. Bake at 375° F for 8 to 10 minutes or until light brown. Cool on cookie sheet for 1 minute; remove to wire rack to cool completely.

Janeyce Michel-Cupito, Powderpuff Barbeque

CHOCOLATE CHIP COOKIES

Yield: 112 servings

5	cups rolled oats	2	cups packed brown sugar
4	cups flour	4	eggs
2	teaspoons baking powder	2	teaspoons vanilla extract
2	teaspoons baking soda	4	cups chocolate chips
1	teaspoon salt	1	(8-ounce) chocolate candy
2	cups butter, softened		bar, grated
2	cups sugar		

Process oats in blender or food processor until powdery. Combine with flour, baking powder, baking soda and salt in bowl; mix well. Cream butter, sugar and brown sugar in mixer bowl until smooth. Add eggs and vanilla; mix well. Add oat mixture; mix well. Stir in chocolate chips and grated chocolate. Shape into balls. Place 2 inches apart on lightly greased cookie sheet. Bake at 375° F for 6 minutes. Remove to wire rack to cool.

Sherry Russell

Dave and Sherry Russell, of the Russellers' Chuck Wagon team of Pleasant Hill, Missouri, are two-time Grand Champions at the Blue Springs' Blaze-Off in Blue Springs, Missouri. These cookies have earned Sherry many compliments.

'Que Tip

History books state the heaviest hog ever recorded was a Poland China hog named "Big Bill" weighing 2,552 pounds and measuring nine feet long, with a belly that dragged the ground. The hog was owned by Burford Butler of Jackson, Tennessee, in 1933.

CHOCOLATE-CHOCOLATE CHIP COOKIES

Yield: 36 servings

½ cup butter
4 ounces unsweetened chocolate, chopped
1½ cups semisweet chocolate chips
4 eggs
1½ cups sugar
2 teaspoons vanilla extract

1½ cups flour
½ teaspoon baking powder
½ teaspoon salt
2 cups chopped toasted pecans
1½ cups semisweet chocolate chips

Line 2 cookie sheets with parchment paper or waxed paper. Heat butter, unsweetened chocolate and 1½ cups chocolate chips in saucepan until blended, stirring frequently. Cool slightly. Beat eggs, sugar and vanilla in mixer bowl until blended. Add mixture of flour, baking powder and salt; mix well. Add to chocolate mixture; mix well. Stir in pecans and 1½ cups chocolate chips. Drop by rounded 2 tablespoonfuls 1 inch apart onto prepared cookie sheets. Bake at 350° F for 10 minutes or until cookies are cracked and shiny. Cool slightly on cookie sheets before removing to cooling racks.

Janeyce Michel-Cupito, Powderpuff Barbeque

'Que Tip

Place meat in the smoker when the temperature reaches 300° F. Then cook at a temperature between 200° F and 220° F. This will sear the meat and seal in the juices.

WHOOPIE PIES

Yield: 18 servings

2 cups flour	½ cup butter, softened
1 cup sugar	½ cup shortening
5 tablespoons baking cocoa	1 cup marshmallow creme
1½ teaspoons baking soda	1 teaspoon vanilla extract
1 cup milk	1 cup confectioners' sugar
1 egg, beaten	
5 tablespoons margarine, softened	

Combine flour, sugar, baking cocoa and baking soda in bowl; mix well. Add milk, egg and margarine, beating until blended. Drop by teaspoonfuls onto ungreased cookie sheet. Bake at 350° F for 10 to 15 minutes or until edges are crisp. Remove to wire rack to cool. Beat butter, shortening and marshmallow creme in mixer bowl until creamy. Add vanilla, beating until blended. Add confectioners' sugar. Beat for 2 minutes, scraping bowl occasionally. Spread over half the cookies; top with remaining cookies.

Donna McClure, P.D.T. (Pretty Damn Tasty)

'Que Tip

Test meat for doneness by making a small cut into the center of the meat. Remember that smoking may leave a bright pink ring just beneath the browned surface. Or use a meat thermometer to check the internal temperature of the meat at the end of the smoking or cooking process.

APPLE CAKE

Yield: 15 servings

1³⁄₄ cups sugar	2 teaspoons cinnamon
1 cup vegetable oil	1 teaspoon baking soda
3 eggs	4 unpeeled apples, chopped
2 cups flour	¹⁄₄ cup confectioners' sugar

Beat sugar, oil and eggs in bowl until blended. Add sifted mixture of flour, cinnamon and baking soda; mix well. Fold in apples. Spoon into greased and floured 9x13-inch cake pan. Bake at 350° F for 35 to 40 minutes or until cake tests done. Sprinkle with confectioners' sugar.

John & Sue Beadle, B.S. Cookers

FRESH APPLE CAKE WITH CARAMEL ICING

Yield: 16 servings

3 eggs	1 teaspoon baking soda
1¹⁄₄ cups vegetable oil	¹⁄₂ teaspoon cinnamon
2 cups sugar	¹⁄₂ teaspoon nutmeg
1 teaspoon vanilla extract	1 cup packed brown sugar
3 cups chopped peeled apples	¹⁄₂ cup butter
	¹⁄₄ cup evaporated milk
3 cups flour	¹⁄₂ teaspoon vanilla extract
1 teaspoon salt	

Beat eggs in mixer bowl until frothy. Add oil, sugar and 1 teaspoon vanilla; mix well. Stir in apples. Mix in sifted mixture of flour, salt, baking soda, cinnamon and nutmeg. Spoon into greased and floured tube pan. Place in cold oven. Bake at 325° F for 45 minutes. Cool. Invert onto serving platter. Bring brown sugar, butter, evaporated milk and ¹⁄₂ teaspoon vanilla to a boil in saucepan. Boil for 3 to 4 minutes, stirring frequently. Remove from heat. Beat with wooden spoon until of spreading consistency. Spread over top and side of cake.

Melody Morgan, Vienna Volunteer Fire Department Cooking Team

CARROT CAKE

Yield: 16 servings

2 cups sifted flour	1 cup chopped pecans
2 teaspoons baking powder	1 cup raisins
2 teaspoons cinnamon	1 (1-pound) package
1 teaspoon baking soda	confectioners' sugar
1 teaspoon salt	8 ounces cream cheese,
1¼ cups corn oil	softened
2 cups sugar	1 cup butter, softened
4 eggs	1 teaspoon vanilla extract
1 pound carrots, grated	

Sift flour, baking powder, cinnamon, baking soda and salt together. Beat corn oil and sugar in mixer bowl until blended. Add ½ of the dry ingredients; mix well. Add remaining dry ingredients alternately with eggs, mixing well after each addition. Stir in carrots, pecans and raisins. Spoon into lightly oiled angel food cake pan. Bake at 325° F for 1 hour and 10 minutes. Cool in upright pan on wire rack. Invert cake onto plate; slice horizontally into 2 layers. Beat confectioners' sugar, cream cheese, butter and vanilla in mixer bowl until of spreading consistency, scraping bowl occasionally. Place 1 cake layer on serving platter; spread with some of cream cheese frosting. Top with remaining cake layer. Spread top and side of cake with remaining cream cheese frosting. May sprinkle with toasted coconut.

Janeyce Michel-Cupito, Powderpuff Barbeque

'Que Tip

In ancient China, fresh pork enjoyed royal status. Around 4000 B.C., the Chinese people were ordered to raise and breed hogs—by a royal decree from the Emperor of China.

WHOLE WHEAT CARROT CAKE
Yield: 12 servings

2	cups whole wheat flour	3	cups finely shredded carrots
1	tablespoon toasted wheat germ	1	cup chopped pecans
1	teaspoon baking powder	8	ounces cream cheese, softened
1	teaspoon baking soda		
1	teaspoon salt	½	cup butter or margarine, softened
1	teaspoon cinnamon		
1¼	cups honey	2	cups confectioners' sugar
½	cup melted butter	1	teaspoon vanilla extract
1	teaspoon molasses	½	teaspoon molasses or honey
1	teaspoon vanilla extract		
4	eggs	¼	cup chopped pecans

Combine flour, wheat germ, baking powder, baking soda, salt and cinnamon in mixer bowl; mix well. Add honey, melted butter, 1 teaspoon molasses and 1 teaspoon vanilla. Beat at low speed until blended. Add eggs 1 at a time, beating well after each addition. Stir in carrots and 1 cup pecans. Spoon into 2 greased round cake pans. Bake at 350° F for 30 to 35 minutes or until layers test done. Cool in pans for 10 minutes. Remove to wire rack to cool completely. Beat cream cheese and softened butter in mixer bowl until smooth. Add confectioners' sugar, 1 teaspoon vanilla and ½ teaspoon molasses, beating until blended. Stir in ¼ cup pecans. Spread between layers and over top and side of cake. May delete molasses in cake batter. May bake in greased bundt pan.

Donna McClure, P.D.T. (Pretty Damn Tasty)

PUMPKIN BUNDT CAKE

Yield: 16 servings

2 cups flour	4 ounces cream cheese, softened
2 cups sugar	
2 teaspoons cinnamon	¼ cup butter, softened
2 teaspoons baking soda	2½ cups confectioners' sugar
½ teaspoon salt	¼ (to ⅓) cup chopped pecans
4 eggs, beaten	
1 cup vegetable oil	
2 cups canned pumpkin, puréed	

Combine flour, sugar, cinnamon, baking soda and salt in bowl; mix well. Stir in eggs, oil and pumpkin. Spoon into greased and floured bundt pan. Bake at 350° F for 55 minutes. Let stand until cool. Invert onto serving plate. Spread top with mixture of cream cheese, butter and confectioners' sugar, allowing frosting to drizzle down side slightly; sprinkle with pecans.

Libby Hayes

'Que Tip

For variety, add chopped smoked brisket instead of smoked ham to beans or peas, add brisket to rice dishes, to chile con queso along with chopped avocado, fold into an omelet, add to your favorite marinara sauce, or substitute brisket for chicken in your favorite chicken dish.

APPLE CREAM PIE

Yield: 6 servings

1½ cups sour cream	½ cup flour
1 cup sugar	⅓ cup packed brown sugar
¼ cup flour	⅓ cup sugar
1 egg	1 tablespoon cinnamon
2 teaspoons vanilla extract	Salt to taste
¾ teaspoon salt	½ cup chilled butter
3 pounds cooking apples, peeled, sliced	1 cup coarsely chopped walnuts
1 unbaked (10-inch) pie shell	

Combine sour cream, 1 cup sugar, ¼ cup flour, egg, vanilla and ¾ teaspoon salt in bowl; mix well. Stir in apples. Spoon into pie shell. Cover edges loosely with foil. Bake at 450° F for 35 to 40 minutes or until bubbly. Combine ½ cup flour, brown sugar, ⅓ cup sugar, cinnamon and salt to taste in bowl; mix well. Cut in butter until crumbly. Stir in walnuts. Remove pie from oven; discard foil. Sprinkle crumb mixture over pie. Bake for 15 minutes longer.

Sharon Allen

'Que Tip

When barbequing for a long period of time, place
ten to twelve briquettes around the outer edge of the hot
coals when you start cooking. These may then be placed
in the cooking area as needed.

BANANA CARAMEL PIE

Yield: 8 servings

1 (14-ounce) can sweetened condensed milk	1 baked (9-inch) pie shell
4 (or 5) medium bananas, sliced	¼ cup chopped walnuts
	4 cups whipped topping
	¼ cup chopped walnuts

Pour condensed milk into pie plate; cover with foil. Place in hot water bath. Bake at 425° F for 1 hour or until thick and caramel colored. Arrange bananas in pie shell. Pour caramelized condensed milk over bananas; sprinkle with ¼ cup walnuts. Mound with whipped topping; sprinkle with ¼ cup walnuts. Chill until serving time. Prepare and serve same day for best quality.

Ivan "Sam" Houston, Salt City Sizzlers

MILLION DOLLAR PIE

Yield: 8 servings

1 cup flour	1 cup sugar
½ cup melted butter	1 (20-ounce) can crushed pineapple, drained
1 cup broken pecans	1 cup broken pecans
8 ounces cream cheese, softened	16 ounces whipped topping

Combine flour and butter in bowl; mix well. Stir in 1 cup pecans. Pat over bottom and side of pie plate. Bake at 350° F for 20 minutes. Let stand until cool. Beat cream cheese and sugar in mixer bowl until smooth. Stir in pineapple and 1 cup pecans. Fold in whipped topping. Spoon into pie shell. Chill until serving time.

Sandra Roming, Meat Tenders

Larry and Sandra Roming, of the Meat Tenders team of Eddy, Texas, are heavily involved with the Central Texas Barbecue Association.

PEANUT BUTTER PIE

Yield: 8 servings

¾ cup sifted confectioners' sugar	3 egg yolks, slightly beaten
⅓ cup peanut butter	2 tablespoons butter
1 baked (9-inch) pie shell	1 teaspoon vanilla extract
½ cup sugar	3 egg whites
⅓ cup flour	½ teaspoon cream of tartar
⅛ teaspoon salt	½ cup sugar
2 cups milk, scalded	1 teaspoon cornstarch

Combine confectioners' sugar and peanut butter in bowl, stirring until crumbly. Sprinkle over bottom of pie shell. Combine ½ cup sugar, flour and salt in double boiler. Stir in milk. Cook over boiling water until thickened, stirring constantly. Stir a small amount of hot mixture into egg yolks; stir egg yolks into hot mixture. Cook for several minutes or until of the desired consistency, stirring constantly. Stir in butter and vanilla. Spoon into prepared pie shell. Let stand until cool. Beat egg whites in mixer bowl until foamy. Add cream of tartar, beating until soft peaks form. Add mixture of ½ cup sugar and cornstarch gradually, beating constantly until shiny and stiff peaks form. Spread over prepared layers. Bake at 325° F for 10 to 15 minutes or until light brown. Let stand until cool.

Tom & Nancy Wallace, Lone Wolf Cookers

Tom and Nancy Wallace of the Lone Wolf Cookers team are proprietors of Lone Wolf BBQ Restaurant in Mankato, Minnesota.

'Que Tip

The ancient Chinese were so averse to being separated from fresh pork that the dead were sometimes accompanied to the grave with their herd of hogs.

SPECIAL PIE

Yield: 6 servings

3 extra-large egg yolks	1 unbaked (9-inch) pie shell
1½ cups sour cream	1 cup semisweet chocolate
1 cup sugar	chips
1 tablespoon flour	3 extra-large egg whites
1 teaspoon vanilla extract	¼ teaspoon cream of tartar
⅛ teaspoon salt	½ cup sugar

Beat egg yolks in mixer bowl until lemon-colored. Add sour cream, 1 cup sugar, flour, vanilla and salt. Beat for 3 minutes, scraping bowl occasionally. Spoon into pie shell. Bake at 400° F for 5 minutes. Reduce oven temperature to 275° F. Bake until set. Remove from oven. Sprinkle with chocolate chips. Cool on wire rack. Beat egg whites in mixer bowl until foamy. Add cream of tartar, beating until soft peaks form. Add ½ cup sugar, beating constantly until stiff peaks form. Spread over pie, sealing to edge. Bake at 325° F for 10 to 15 minutes or until light brown. Chill until serving time.

Lee Ann Cifers-Tabb

Lee Ann Cifers-Tabb of Atlanta, Georgia, shares her grandmother Elmira's Special Pie recipe with us. Elmira died in May, 1994, at the age of one hundred. Her legacy lives on with this wonderful dessert!

'Que Tip

In order to keep a constant temperature, it is preferable to put small, rather than large, pieces of wood chunks in the fire.

ETCETERA

Competition Barbequing

There is a phenomenon emerging on the barbeque scene—The Barbeque Contest. Never heard of such a thing, you say. Well, you read it first here. Ten years ago, there were fewer than 100 barbeque contests in the United States. In 1995, there were more than 400 of which we know. We suspect there are numerous small-town community and charity events not connected with any of the contest-sanctioning organizations.

What is this animal? It is an event, usually sponsored as a community awareness festival or charity fund raiser, in which teams pit their barbeque cooking skills against one another. They compete for prize money, ribbons, or trophies, and bragging rights against their fellow pitmasters.

Who Competes and Why?

A couple of good-ole-boys are sitting around one night putting away a few brews. The subject of the American Royal Barbecue Contest comes up. Sam mentions to George that his co-worker, the K.C. Rib Doctor, is entered in the Royal. Sam and George drop by and sample the Rib Doctor's ribs, and experience the flavor of the event—blues, jazz, team parties, the spectacle. On the way home, Sam says his ribs can beat the Rib Doctor's ribs any day. George says "put your money where your mouth is." Sam says okay, but he can't do it alone. Would George help? George allows as to how that might be fun—they could call themselves the Can Benders! Voila, a team is born.

They check their KCBS news, *The Bullsheet,* to search out the next contest. They don't win any prizes the first time, but have a great time. Now they're more determined than ever to get it exactly right. The team expands, duties are delegated, and everyone has a great time. They're hooked.

The simple fact of the matter is that this is a sport in which anyone can compete. You don't have to be independently wealthy—your equipment and supplies can be as simple or elaborate as you can afford. No special training is required—just practice, practice, practice—and you always get to eat. It is a sport in which no special stamina is required other than being willing to get up during the night and tend the fire. It's camping out with your family and friends, visiting new places to cook in events, fine tuning your cooking skills, and having a great time.

Who Sponsors Barbeque Contests?

The city of Kearney, Missouri, has a community festival named Jesse James Days. Larry Pratt, festival chairperson thought a barbeque contest would be a great tie-in to the festival. He petitioned for KCBS sanction. The first year his contest drew twenty-four teams. The festival had about 5,000 attendees. The eighth year, 1994, the contest had fifty teams, and the festival drew 25,000.

The American Royal Barbecue Contest was created as a fund raiser for the American Royal Association, producers of one of the oldest and largest horse show and livestock competitions in the United States. The Barbecue didn't make a lot of money the first few years, but the event continued to grow and prosper. Besides, barbeque is a strong part of Kansas City's cultural heritage. Through the hard work (all unpaid) of the Barbecue Contest Committee, volunteers, and coordinators, the event has grown to the largest barbeque contest in the world—with more than 280 teams competing in an average of eight categories, with more than 500 judges, and a world-class barbeque weekend. The American Royal Barbecue Contest is now the largest fund raiser for the American Royal Horse and Livestock Show. The Barbecue Contest was dubbed "The World Series of Barbecue" by CBS Sunday Morning star Bill Geist. It is great for community awareness and for the Kansas City economy.

To Sanction or Not to Sanction?

There are presently seven groups throughout the United States that sanction (officiate) barbeque contests. Since this is a KCBS book, we'll only discuss KCBS sanction.

"KCBS Sanctioned" means that the contest sponsor agrees to abide by the Rules and Regulations of the Kansas City Barbeque Society. It means they will guarantee the purse, if any. It means that they will have KCBS Contest Representatives present to officiate the contest. It means they won't have to reinvent the wheel, because we've already made all the mistakes that can be made, and have learned not only what to do, but also what not to do. It gives the sponsors a built-in base of cooking teams from which to draw. For the cooking teams, it gives the assurance that the contest will be administered in strict accordance with KCBS Rules and Regulations. Those regulations have been developed by members of cooking teams and ratified by the KCBS Board of Directors. Finally, it means that the awards will be announced on that day, rather than at some unspecified point in the future.

The KCBS Judging System is "Blind Judging Only." That means that samples are placed in a 9x9-inch hinged undivided styrofoam container with a team number on top. The samples are renumbered by a KCBS Contest Official and sent to the judging tent. They are judged by six judges, many of whom are KCBS Certified. This system insures that judges knowing their friends' team number on the outside will not know whose meat they are judging after the containers have been renumbered. The judges rate the meat on a scale of 1 (spit it out-disgusting) to 9 (heavenly) on the criteria of appearance, tenderness/texture, and taste. The judging slips are picked up by a Table Captain and delivered to the tabulation area. A tabulator enters the scores. The state-of-the-art computer program automatically doubles the taste score (most important criterion) and drops the low score (you might have a prima donna judge). It then compiles the data and a winner by category is determined. The category scores are merged and a grand champion based on total cumulative points is determined.

In KCBS-sanctioned contests, the categories are pork ribs (spareribs or baby backs), chicken, pork (butt or shoulder), and beef brisket. Other categories may be added at the option of the sponsor. Steak or shellfish categories, i.e., grilled items, may not count toward grand champion.

What Happens at a Barbeque Contest?

It's a campout, party, and competition—all rolled into one. You pack up the tent, cooker, meat, and supplies; load up the kids, and off to the cookoff. Usually Friday is set-up day and party, then Saturday the competition. The cookers visit with each other and make new friends. Often the Friday evening informal dinners are gastronomic delights. Then comes the trimming and rubbing the brisket, skinning the ribs, and marinating the pork in preparation for the competition. Saturday is Judgment Day. The meats are presented for judging by category at the specified time, ribs at noon, chicken at 12:30, pork at 1:00, brisket at 1:30, and so on. Awards are announced. The teams pack up and go home, hit the shower, eat ice cream (BSP—Barbeque Saturation Point has been reached long ago), and go to bed. Sunday is spent unpacking and washing pans in the backyard, but hopefully there will be a ribbon or trophy to make the cleanup chores more palatable. At any rate, it was an enjoyable weekend with friends and family.

For the sponsor it means that awareness of their community, festival, event, or fund raiser is heightened. Hopefully, they will have raised money. The public will have come out and sampled some barbeque and experienced a real slice of Americana.

If you are considering sponsoring such an event, write or call KCBS for a Rules and Regulations book. It covers the requirements for a sanctioned contest. Be prepared for a lot of hard work, but a very rewarding experience. (Note: Most first-year contests can only hope to break even. Be prepared to make the financial and time investment required for growth and success.)

For the interested spectator, this is your chance to experience the sights, sounds, and smells of competition cooking. You might be lucky enough to sample some great 'Que. You can chat with the cookers (except when they are preparing samples for judging) and might be able to pick up a few tips on cooking. You'll see rigs you never dreamed of—from a Cessna airplane turned cooker complete with meat seeking missiles, to a giant Armadillo cooker named Bubba.

We hope this section has at least whetted your appetite to experience a barbeque competition.

Contests

As noted in previous sections, The Barbeque Contest phenomenon is exploding. As usual, KCBS is in the thick of things sanctioning (officiating) events. Following is a listing by month of KCBS Sanctioned Events. The public is encouraged to attend these community festivals. Call the coordinator in advance to confirm date, location, and schedule.

April

KCBS Spring Training, Bucyrus, KS. Contact: KCBS, 11514 Hickman Mills Drive, Kansas City, MO 64134, (816) 765-5891.

Oklahoma Land Run, Oklahoma City, OK. Contact: Dale Hamilton, 700 N.E. 13th St., Oklahoma City, OK 73104, (405) 271-6601.

Mid-South Regional Barbeque Championship, Lincoln, AR. Contact: Don Rose, P.O. Box 837, Lincoln, AR 72744, (501) 824-5645.

May

Old Town Bar-B-Que Cookoff, Wichita, KS. Contact: Stacey Boyd, 350 W. Douglas, Wichita, KS 67202, (316) 268-1130.

Blue Devil Barbecue Cookoff (Sunflower State Championship) and Annual Kansas State Novice Barbecue Championship, Kansas City, KS. Contact: Karen Atchley, KCKCC Endowment Association, 7250 State Avenue, Kansas City, KS 66212, (913) 596-9632.

Funfest "Lookin' for a Cookin'," Archie, MO. Contact: Mick Lethcho, 6 Hiview Ridge, Archie, MO 64725, (816) 430-5273.

Crooked Creek Crawdad Days Barbeque Cookoff, Harrison, AR. Contact: Dennis Daniels or Tom Arnold, P.O. Box 939, Harrison, AR 72602-0939, (501) 741-2659.

Raytown BBQ Cookoff, Raytown, MO. Contact: Quentin E. Clark, 9715 E. 63rd St., Raytown, MO 64133, (816) 356-0505.

Oklahoma Joe's Interplanetary BBQ Championship, Stillwater, OK. Contact: Joe Davidson, 1616 Airport Road, Stillwater, OK 75075, (405) 377-3080.

June

North Kansas City BBQ Contest-MO State Championship, North Kansas City, MO. Contact: John or Suzi Cliff, 3735 N. Walrond, Kansas City, MO 64117, (816) 452-5199.

McLouth Prairie Days BBQ Blowout-N.E. Kansas State Championship, McLouth, KS. Contact: Marlin McAfterty, P.O. Box 116, McLouth, KS 66054, (913) 796-6112 or (913) 796-6737.

Krehbiel's Appreciation Days BBQ Contest, McPherson, KS. Contact: Homer Krehbiel, Rt. 3, Box 115, McPherson, KS 67460, (316) 241-0103 or (316) 241-6565.

CONTESTS

Blue Ridge Barbecue and Music Festival, Tryon, NC. Contact: Jim Tabb, Tryon Chamber of Commerce, 401 N. Trade St., Tryon, NC 28782, (704) 859-6236.

Stockyard Stampede Festival Chili & BBQ Cookoff, Oklahoma City, OK. Contact: Chris Wilson, 2501 Exchange Ave., Room 118, Oklahoma City, OK 73108, (405) 235-7267.

The Great Pork BarbeQlossal, Des Moines, IA. Contact: Anne Rehnstrom, National Pork Producers Council, P.O. Box 10383, Des Moines, IA 50306, (515) 223-2622.

Greater Slater Open BBQ Cookoff, Slater, MO. Contact: Bud Summers, P.O. Box 100, 201 N. Main, Slater, MO 65349, (816) 529-2222.

Grain Valley BBQ Contest, Grain Valley, MO. Contact: Sharon Stewart, P.O. Box 447, Grain Valley, MO 64029, (816) 229-2875.

BBQ & Boats, Smithville, MO. Contact: Cheryl Parker, 4010 N.E. Antioch Road, Kansas City, MO 64117, (816) 452-5246.

Lexington BBQ Bail-Out, Lexington, MO. Contact: Bill Rousseau, P.O. Box 714, Grain Valley, MO 64029, (816) 229-2225.

Cole Younger Days Bar-B-Que Cookoff, Lee's Summit, MO. Contact: Lee's Summit Chamber of Commerce, 342 S.W. Blue Parkway, Lee's Summit, MO 64063, Mike Coupe (816) 246-6776.

The Great Lenexa Barbecue Battle-Kansas State Championship, Lenexa, KS. Contact: Bill Nicks, Lenexa Parks and Recreation, 13420 Oak St., Lenexa, KS 66215, (913) 541-8492.

Chief Osceola Bar-B-Que "Smoke Out," Osceola, MO. Contact: Cecil Pritchett, Box J, 760 2nd St., Osceola, MO 64776, (417) 646-9216.

July

Zed Martin BBQ Contest, Platte City, MO. Contact: Donna Van Fosson, 13100 Bethel Terrace, Platte City, MO 64079, (816) 858-2028.

Illinois State Championship, W. Chicago, IL. Contact: Jim Burns, 1200 W. Hawthorne, W. Chicago, IL 60185, (708) 231-6262.

Cherokee Strip Chili & Bar-B-Que Cookoff, Ponca City, OK. Contact: Debbie Whitener, 3624 Wellington, Ponca City, OK 74604, (405) 767-1698.

MidWest Regional Championship Barbeque & Blues Fest, Gladstone, MO. Contact: Robert Hacker, Gladstone Area Chamber of Commerce, P.O. Box 10751, Gladstone, MO 64188-0751, (816) 436-4523.

Platte County Fair, Tracy, MO. Contact: Brad Babcock, 16725 136th St., Platte City, MO 64079, (816) 741-8328.

Elk's Payne County BBQ Blazathon, Stillwater, OK. Contact: The Elks Lodge, 202 E. McElroy, Stillwater, OK 74075, Pat Pittman, (405) 372-3925 or Brad Oliver, (405) 372-4118.

Piper B-B-Q Cook-Off, Bonner Springs, KS. Contact: Craig Howell, 12117 Leavenworth Road, Kansas City, KS 66109, (913) 721-1163.

Contests

Dodge City Days Barbeque Contest, Dodge City, KS. Contact: Gretchen Woolsey, P.O. Box 939, Dodge City, KS 67801, (316) 227-3119.

Kay County BBQ & Chili Cook-Off, Blackwell, OK. Contact: DeWayne Muret, Route 1, Box 156, Newkirk, OK 74647, (405) 363-3394.

KFDI Barbecue Fest, Wichita, KS. Contact: Kathleen Wille, P.O. Box 1402, Wichita, KS 67201, (316) 838-9141.

Jamesport B-B-Q Cook-Off, Jamesport, MO. Contact: Janet DenHartog, Jamesport Community Association, Box 215, Jamesport, MO 64648, (816) 684-6711.

August

Village of Laurie Annual BBQ Cookoff, Laurie, MO. Contact: Shirley Jobe, P.O. Box 1054, Laurie, MO 65038, (314) 374-8776.

Arkansas Championship Wild Hog Bar-B-Que Cookoff, Holiday Island, AR. Contact: Willie Nemec, 1 Landing Drive, Holiday Island-Eureka Springs, AR 72632, (501) 253-7561.

Bates County BBQ Championship, Butler, MO. Contact: Harlan Hartley, (816) 679-6236 or Butler Area Chamber of Commerce, 17 S. Delaware, Butler, MO 64730, (816) 679-3380.

Michigan State Championship, Grand Rapids, MI. Contact: John Beadle, 6843 Adaside, Ada, MI 49301, (616) 676-2164.

The Woodlands Barbeque Cook-Off, Kansas City, KS. Contact: Jill Walton, c/o The Woodlands, 9700 Leavenworth Road, Kansas City, KS 66112, (913) 299-9797.

Johnson County Fair BBQ, Olathe, KS. Contact: Doc Wollen, 180 E. Cedar, Olathe, KS 66061, (913) 782-0188.

City of Cookeville Cookoff, sponsored by Crimestoppers, Cookeville, TN. Contact: Leonard Livingston, P.O. Box 966, Cookeville, TN 38503, (615) 537-9092.

September

Blue Springs Barbeque Blaze-Off State Championship Contest, Blue Springs, MO. Contact: Pam Buck, City of Blue Springs, 903 Main St., Blue Springs, MO 64015, (816) 228-0137.

Benton County Fair Cookoff, Ashland, MS. Contact: Benton County Fair Association, P.O. Box 158, Ashland, MS 38603, (601) 224-8932.

Hog Wild for Kids, Gibsonville, NC. Contact: Jim Mason, 50 Driftwood Court, Gibsonville, NC 27249, (800) 222-7566 x3538 or (910) 449-4551.

Jesse James Barbeque Cook Out, Kearney, MO. Contact: Larry Pratt, P.O. Box 202, Kearney, MO 64060, (816) 628-4502 or (816) 274-8580.

State Barbeque Championship of Nebraska, Omaha, NE. Contact: Dale Drake, Greater Omaha Barbeque Society, 1215 N. 101st Circle, Omaha, NE 68114, (402) 393-4376.

October

American Royal Barbecue Contests, Kansas City, MO. Contact: Pam McKee, American Royal Association, 1701 American Royal Court, Kansas City, MO 64102, (816) 221-9800.

Pig and Pepper Festival, Westford, MA. Contact: Bob Rothenberg, c/o Carlisle Education Foundation, P.O. Box 734, Carlisle, MA 01741, (508) 369-0366.

Mountain Mania Barbeque Cook-Off & Festival, Mountain Home, AR. Contact: Richard Vollmer, Peoples Bank, P.O. Box B, Mountain Home, AR 72653, (501) 425-2166.

Old Shawnee Town BBQ Contest, Shawnee, KS. Contact: Terry M. Lodge, City of Shawnee, 13817 Johnson Drive, Shawnee, KS 66216, (913) 631-5200.

Jack Daniel's World Championship Barbecue Contest, Lynchburg, TN. (By Invitation Only). Contact: Tana Shupe, Jack Daniel's, 110 21st Ave. South, Nashville, TN 37203, (615) 340-1065.

November

Florida State BBQ Championship Contest, Bradenton, FL. Contact: John Abbuhl, Kirby Stewart Post 24, American Legion, 2000 75th St. West, Bradenton, FL 34209, (813) 794-3489.

Resource Guide

Associations

Barbecue Industry Association, (708) 369-2404, 710 E. Ogden, Suite 113, Naperville, IL 60540

National Barbecue Association, (704) 365-3622, fax (704) 365-3678, 723 S. Sharon Amity Rd., Suite 214, Charlotte, NC 28211

Books/Publications

Chile Pepper, (505) 266-8322, fax (505) 266-2127, 5106 Grand N.E., Albuquerque, NM 87108

Culinary Institute of Smoke-Cooking, (314) 335-7869, 2323 Brookwood, Box 163, Cape Girardeau, MO 64702-0163

Goat Gap Gazette, (713) 667-4652, fax (713) 644-3708, P.O. Box 271299, Houston, TX 77277-1299

Kansas City Barbeque Society, (816) 765-5891, fax (816) 765-5860, 11514 Hickman Mills Dr., Kansas City, MO 64134

National Barbecue News, (912) 384-0001, P.O. Box 981, Douglas, GA 31533

Pig Out Publications, Inc., (816) 531-3119, fax (816) 531-6113, 4245 Walnut, Kansas City, MO 64111

Smoke in Yer Eye Publications, (918) 256-5198, P.O. Box 426, Vinita, OK 74301

Sauces, Seasonings, Rubs, Spices, and Salsas

All-American Bar-B-Que Company, Inc., (913) 649-6388, 7607 Fairway, Prairie Village, KS 66208

All Cajun Food Company, (800) 467-3613 or (318) 332-3612, fax (318) 332-1467, 1019 Delcambre Rd., Breaux Bridge, LA 70517

Ashley Food Company, Inc.-Mad Dog BBQ Sauces, (800) 61-SAUCE, (167) 783-0565, fax (617) 783-5858, 1085 Commonwealth Avenue, Ste. 306, Boston, MA 02215

BBQ Champs-MasterFood Specialties, Inc., (800) 39COOKIN, P.O. Box 1246, Houston, TX 77251

Bilardo Brothers Food Specialties, Inc., (816) 943-1091, fax (816) 942-1338, P.O. Box 15586, Kansas City, MO 64106

Billy Bones BBQ, (517) 832-2922, 4326 N. Saginaw Rd., Midland, MI 48640

Boardroom Bar-B-Q Sauce of the Month Club, (913) 642-6273, fax (913) 642-2469, 9600 Antioch, Overland Park, KS 66210

Chef Dan's, Inc., (913) 362-1361, 10103 Johnson Dr., Merriam, KS 66203

Cimarron Doc's Bar-B-Que & Chili Co., (913) 897-6443, P.O. Box 23065, Shawnee Mission, KS 66223

Cockrell General Store, (816) 697-3611, 30003 E. Old U.S. Hwy. 50, Lee's Summit, MO 64086

El Paso Chile Co., (915) 544-3434, fax (915) 544-7552, 909 Texas Ave., El Paso, TX 79901

Flower of the Flames, (913) 492-1414, 14406 W. 100th St., Lenexa, KS 66215

Fast Eddy's, (816) 741-1294, 7621 N.W. Milrey, Kansas City, MO 64152

Great Southern Sauce Company, (800) 43-SAUCE or (501) 663-3338, 5705 Kavanaugh, Little Rock, AR 72207

Ham I Am!, (800) 742-6426 or (214) 238-1776, fax (214) 238-1764, 1303 Columbia Dr., Suite 201, Richardson, TX 75081

Happy "Holla" Bar-B-Q, (913) 268-7828, P.O. Box 822, Shawnee Mission, KS 66201

Harley's Texas Style Bar-B-Que Seasoning, (800) 573-9070 or (409) 542-3281, fax (409) 542-1630, Route 3, Box 781, Giddings, TX 78942

Head Country, (405) 762-9882, P.O. Box 2324, Ponca City, OK 74602

Hunt Marckwald's Gourmet Foods, Inc., (516) 288-6600, 15 Hazelwood Ave., Westhampton Beach, NY 11978

J-Bar-J, (314) 348-1529, Route 2, Box 2300, Osage Beach, MO 65065

K-Cass Bar-B-Que Food Products, (816) 540-3703, 17720 S. Merriott Rd., Pleasant Hill, MO 64080

K. C. Baron of Barbecue Sauces, (913) 262-6029, 3625 W. 50th Terr. Roeland Park, KS 66205

K. C. Rib Doctor, (913) 268-6115, 14004 W. 69th St., Shawnee, KS 66215

Kingsfords, Inc., (800) 357-8057 or (913) 441-8057, 24052 W. 63rd St., Shawnee Mission, KS 66226

Lazy L Smokers BBQ Sauce, (314) 965-8910, fax (314) 256-3197, P.O. Box 31394, Des Peres, MO 63131

Marty's Bar-B-Q, (816) 453-2222, 2516 N.E. Vivion Rd., Kansas City, MO 64118

Mr. Z's, (913) 649-6637, 9507 Beverly, Overland Park, KS 66207

Obie-Cue's Texas Spices, (214) 943-9974 (fax & phone), 1826 Enchanted Ln., Lancaster, TX 75146

Oklahoma Joe's, (405) 377-3080, P.O. Box 835, Perry, OK 73077

Porky's Gourmet Foods, Inc., (800) PORK-911 or (615) 244-PORK, fax (615) 244-RIBS, P.O. Box 830, Ridgetop, TN 37152

Saucemaster's Gourmet Foods, Inc., (816) 561-7717, 1105 Westport Rd., Kansas City, MO 64111

Two Buddies, (800) 48-SAUCE, fax (805) 985-9967, P.O. Box 68, Port Hueneme, CA 93041

Willingham's, (800) 737-WHAM or (901) 767-9426, fax (901) 767-6759, P.O. Box 17312, Memphis, TN 38187-0312

Cookers

Barbeque & Restaurant Equipment Corp., (800) 280-3463 or (708) 257-5455, fax (708) 484-8818, 26 Keepataw Ct., Lemont, IL 60439-4339

Belson Manufacturing, (800) 323-5664, fax (708) 897-0573, P.O. Box 207, N. Aurora, IL 60542-0207

Benet Gridirons, Inc., (702) 246-0235 or (702) 246-0236, P.O. Box 21941, Carson City, NV 89721

Bierdeman Engineering, "The Drum," (800) DRUM-008, 685 Spread Eagle Dr., Westcliffe, CO 81252-9303

Big John Grills & Rotisseries, (800) 326-9575 or (814) 359-2755, fax (814) 359-2621, P.O. Box 5250, Pleasant Gap, PA 16823

Brinkmann Corp., (800) 527-0717 or (214) 387-4939, fax (800) 780-0109, 4215 McEwen Rd., Dallas, TX 75244

CharBroil, (800) 352-4111, P.O. Box 1240, Columbus, GA 31904-1240

Coleman, (800) 641-9181 or (512) 459-9181, 9070 Research, Burnet Rd., Austin, TX 78758

Cookshack, Inc., (800) 423-0698 or (405) 765-3669, fax (405) 765-2223, 2304 N. Ash St., Ponca City, OK 74601

Enviro Industries, (906) 492-3402, fax (906) 492-3269, 123 Whitefish Point Rd., Paradise, MI 49768

GrillMasters, (305) 591-8011, fax (305) 591-8012, 6324 N.W. 72nd Ave., Miami, FL 33166

GOBLRr Smoke-n-grill, Robert Bishop, (816) 524-3016; Richard Loree, (816) 765-6305

Hasty-Bake, (800) 4AN-OVEN or (918) 665-8220, 7656 E. 46th St., Tulsa, OK 74145

Hickory Creek Bar-B-Q Cooker, (800) 424-8943, fax (901) 664-0978, 1119 Hwy. 45 By-Pass, Jackson, TN 38301

Holstein Manufacturing, (800) 368-4342 or (712) 368-4342, fax (712) 368-2351, 5368 110th St., Holstein, IA 51025

Kansas City Cookers and Grills, (816) 363-8963, 201 E. Bannister Rd., Kansas City, MO 64114

Kingfisher Kountry Kookers, Klingsick's, (405) 375-3710, fax (405) 375-6576, 1107 S. Main, Kingfisher, OK 73750

Klose Fabrications, Inc., (800) 487-7487 or (713) 686-8720, 2214¹/₂ W. 34 St., Houston, TX 77018

Magikitch'n, Inc., (800) 441-1492 or (215) 536-8140, fax (215) 538-3644, 180 Penn Am Dr., Quakertown, PA 18951

Mr. Bar-BQ, (800) 333-2124 or (316) 628-4552, Route 1, Box 175, Canton, KS 67428

New Braunfels Smoker Co. 1, (210) 629-6000, fax (210) 625-8303, Box 3106948, New Braunfels, TX 78131

Oklahoma Joe's, (405) 377-3080, 1616 W. Airport Rd., Stillwater, OK 74075

Old Hickory Pits, (800) 223-9667 or (314) 334-6512, fax (314) 334-3377, 333 N. Main, Cape Girardeau, MO 63701

Pioneer Fabricating, Inc., (800) 262-4303 or (817) 232-4303, fax (817) 232-4306, 1013 Jarvis Road, Ft. Worth, TX 76131

RESOURCE GUIDE

Pyromid, Inc., (800) 824-4288 or (503) 548-1041, 3292 S. Hwy. 97, Redmond, OR 97756

Southern Pride, (800) 851-8180, fax (618) 993-5960 Route 2, Box 21A, Marion, IL 62959

Summit Outdoor Living, (816) 246-8700, 606 N.E. 291 Hwy., Lee's Summit, MO 64086

Swisher-Rotisserie Master, (800) 222-8183, P.O. Box 67, Warrensburg, MO 64093

Traeger Industries, Inc., (800) 872-3437 or (503) 845-9234, fax (503) 845-6366, P.O. Box 829-1385 E. College, Mt. Angel, OR 97362

Ultimate Cooker, (407) 644-6680, fax (407) 644-6840, 803 W. Fairbanks Ave., Winter Park, FL 32789

Willingham's, (800) 737-WHAM or (901) 767-9426, fax (901) 767-6759, P.O. Box 17312, Memphis, TN 38187-0312

Woods

American Wood Products, (800) 223-9046 or (913) 648-7993, fax (913) 648-8019, 9450 Riggs, Overland Park, KS 66212

Chigger Creek Products, (816) 827-4447, 108 Walnut Park Dr., Sedalia, MO 65301

Connecticut Charcoal Co., (203) 227-2101, fax (203) 227-5663, P.O. Box 742, Westport, CT 06881

Fairlane Fireplace Bar-B-Q Wood, (816) 761-1350, 12520 3rd St., Grandview, MO 64030

Nature's Own Charwoods, (800) 289-2427 or (508) 226-4710, fax (508) 226-5210, 453 South Main St., Attleboro, MA 02703

Miscellaneous

Bubba-Q's BBQ Pit Thermometer, Birch Instruments & Controls Co., (800) 662-2183, fax (713) 622-2183, 1221 Austin St., Rosenberg, TX 77471

Charcoal Companion, Inc., (BBQ Accessories), (800) 521-0505, 7955 Edgewater Dr., Oakland, CA 94621

Dayva International, (BBQ Utensils & Accessories), (714) 842-9697, fax (714) 842-5759, 7642 Windfield Dr., Huntington Beach, CA 92647

Exclusively BBQ, (800) 948-1009 or (704) 792-2489, fax (704) 792-2490, 3147 Boy Scout Camp Rd., Kannapolis, NC 28081

GRIL-Del, Inc., (BBQ Accessories), (800) 782-7320 or (507) 632-4281, fax (507) 632-4282, 110-112 W. Main St., P.O. Box 414, Ceylon, MN 56121-0414

Mill-Rose Co., (BBQ Brushes & Accessories), (216) 974-6730, fax (216) 255-5039, 7995 Tyler Blvd., Mentor, OH 44060

Resource Guide

Mr. Bar-B-Q, Inc., (Gas Grill Parts & Accessories), (800) 333-2124 or (516) 752-0670, fax (516) 752-0683, 445 Winding Rd., Old Bethpage, NY 11804

People's Leisure Products, (BBQ Implements), (417) 334-2620, fax (417) 581-7701, 1277 Bee Creek Rd., Branson, MO 65616

S & S Manufacturing, (Canopies and Tents), (800) 397-1159 or (402) 494-4498, 217 W. 26th St., S. Sioux City, NE 68776

Sparkie's Sure Liters, Futures Unlimited, Inc., (316) 326-8906, Wellington, KS 67152

Wolcett & Associates, Inc., (BBQ Sauce & Paraphernalia), (913) 661-9440, 7800 W. 110th St., Overland Park, KS 66210

Instruction

K. C. Baron of Barbecue's School of Pitmasters, (913) 262-6029, 3625 W. 50th Terr., Roeland Park, KS 66205

Happy "Holla" Championship Barbecue Video, (913) 268-7828, P.O. Box 822, Shawnee Mission, KS 66201

Great Chefs, (504) 943-4343, 421 Frenchman St., New Orleans, LA 70116

Kansas City Barbecue Society, (800) 963-5227 or (816) 765-5891, 11514 Hickman Mills Dr., Kansas City, MO 64134

Spectrum Video, "Grilling With Woods" Video, P.O. Box 3669, Cranston, RI 02910

Culinary Institute of Smoke-Cooking, (314) 335-7869, 2323 Brookwood Dr., Cape Girardeau, MO 64701

Nutritional Profiles

The editors have attempted to present these family recipes in a form that allows approximate nutritional values to be computed. Persons with dietary or health problems or whose diets require close monitoring should not rely solely on the nutritional information provided. They should consult their physicians or a registered dietitian for specific information.

Abbreviations for Nutritional Profile

Cal — Calories   Fiber — Dietary Fiber   Sod — Sodium
Prot — Protein   T Fat — Total Fat   g — Grams
Carbo — Carbohydrates   Chol — Cholesterol   mg — Milligrams

Nutritional information for these recipes is computed from information derived from many sources, including materials supplied by the United States Department of Agriculture, computer databanks and journals in which the information is assumed to be in the public domain. However, many specialty items, new products and processed foods may not be available from these sources or may vary from the average values used in these profiles. More information on new and/or specific products may be obtained by reading the nutrient labels. Unless otherwise specified, the nutritional profile of these recipes is based on all measurements being level.

- **Artificial sweeteners** vary in use and strength so should be used "to taste," using the recipe ingredients as a guideline. Sweeteners using aspartame (NutraSweet and Equal) should not be used as a sweetener in recipes involving prolonged heating which reduces the sweet taste. Refer to package information.
- **Alcoholic ingredients** have been analyzed for basic ingredients, although cooking causes the evaporation of alcohol, thus decreasing caloric content.
- **Buttermilk, sour cream** and **yogurt** are the types available commercially.
- **Cake mixes** prepared using package directions include 3 eggs and 1/2 cup oil.
- **Chicken**, cooked for boning and chopping, has been roasted; this method yields the lowest caloric values.
- **Cottage cheese** is cream-style with 4.2% creaming mixture. Dry curd cottage cheese has no creaming mixture.
- **Eggs** are all large. To avoid raw eggs that may carry salmonella as in eggnog or 6-week muffin batter, use an equivalent amount of commercial egg substitute.
- **Flour** is unsifted all-purpose flour.
- **Garnishes**, serving suggestions and other optional additions and variations are not included in the profile.
- **Margarine** and **butter** are regular, not whipped or presoftened.
- **Milk** is whole milk, 3.5% butterfat. Low-fat milk is 1% butterfat. Evaporated milk is whole milk with 60% of the water removed.
- **Oil** is vegetable cooking oil. **Shortening** is hydrogenated vegetable shortening.
- **Salt** and other ingredients to taste as noted in the ingredients have not been included in the nutritional profile.
- If a choice of ingredients has been given, the nutritional profile reflects the first option. If a choice of amounts has been given, the nutritional profile reflects the greater amount.

NUTRITIONAL PROFILES

Pg #	Recipe Title (Approx Per Serving)	Cal	Prot (g)	Carbo (g)	T Fat (g)	% Cal from Fat	Chol (mg)	Sod (mg)
22	Barbequed Whole Hog	Nutritional profile for this recipe is not available.						
23	"Pig Pickin" Barbequed Whole Hog	Nutritional profile for this recipe is not available.						
23	Happy "Holla" Barbequed Smoked Pork	262	29	16	9	31	73	198
24	Maple-Glazed Pork Loin	162	22	6	5	30	55	206
25	Country Boy Pork Tenderloins	295	30	30	5	17	83	507
26	Rosemary Grilled Pork Tenderloins[1]	232	17	12	13	51	46	646
27	Barbequed Pork Butt	239	28	8	10	40	90	1063
27	Carolina-Style Pork Butt	171	21	3	8	42	67	1133
28	Orange-Glazed Pork Butt	214	23	9	9	40	78	799
29	Chinese-Style Barbequed Pork	229	26	7	9	37	73	850
30	Sherry-Glazed Ribs	665	26	44	40	53	104	3547
31	Barbequed Baby Back Ribs	473	38	13	29	57	107	5917
31	Rib Russeller Ribs	442	37	6	29	60	107	2045
32	Barbequed Spareribs	538	29	18	40	65	104	596
32	Blue Ribbon Ribs	419	37	0	29	64	107	2044
33	Smoked Baby Back Ribs	569	37	12	40	65	138	2428
33	Hickory-Flavored Spareribs	363	25	2	26	66	104	1207
34	Marinated Barbequed Spareribs	657	45	14	46	64	182	1249
35	Polynesian Spareribs	613	39	24	40	59	156	2350
35	Tres Colinas Ranch Chinese Barbequed Spareribs[1]	364	21	30	15	38	53	4070
36	Apple-Smoked Pork Chops	321	34	21	11	32	103	85
36	St. Louis Pork Steaks	295	32	13	12	38	90	3555
37	Apple-Glazed Pork Kabobs	494	16	45	29	51	60	1580
38	Pork Butt Hash	214	12	18	11	44	34	29
39	Barbequed Pork Burgers	476	26	36	25	47	80	796
39	Spicy Pork Burgers	261	22	1	18	63	81	403
40	Blue Ribbon Chicken	377	57	0	15	37	176	170
41	Fancy Chicken with Goat Cheese	341	27	1	23	61	79	374
42	Jamaican Jerk Chicken	487	68	7	19	37	201	1908
43	Smokemasters Smoked Chicken	591	60	21	29	45	176	4979
43	Tarragon Butter-Barbequed Chicken	555	51	6	36	59	213	435
44	Orange Chicken	459	50	19	19	37	166	1690
44	Grilled Lemon Chicken	583	50	38	26	40	151	148
45	Honey Dijon Barbequed Chicken	492	50	9	27	49	151	380
45	Carolina Mustard Chicken	221	28	1	11	47	73	409
46	Herb-Smoked Chicken	740	28	62	42	50	73	1589
47	Tequila Chicken[1]	359	28	2	22	54	73	562
48	Wildcat Chicken	566	35	39	23	36	83	2769

NUTRITIONAL PROFILES

Pg #	Recipe Title (Approx Per Serving)	Cal	Prot (g)	Carbo (g)	T Fat (g)	% Cal from Fat	Chol (mg)	Sod (mg)
49	Barbequed Chicken	391	58	3	15	35	176	669
49	Honey-Glazed Chicken	372	44	13	15	38	144	295
50	Cuzin Homer's Chicken Delights	182	16	7	10	48	55	648
51	Oriental Burgers	250	19	32	5	19	36	672
52	Smoked Red Chile-Rubbed Cornish Hens	537	54	1	34	58	174	640
53	Smoked Turkey	523	86	6	15	26	223	206
54	Turkey Meatballs	350	24	11	22	56	110	646
55	Barbequed Brisket	209	28	1	10	43	86	1429
56	Barbequed Beef & Onion Pizza	374	20	33	18	43	57	719
57	Faux Fajitas	375	30	34	13	30	73	751
57	Jalapeño Brisket	202	28	1	8	39	86	184
58	Smoked Barbequed Brisket	224	28	2	10	42	86	878
59	Tri-Tip Roast	261	22	3	18	62	64	35
60	Shrimp-Stuffed Beef Roast	233	32	1	10	41	121	126
61	Chateaubriand en Pâté	258	27	1	15	55	250	194
61	Grilled Beef Tenderloin[1]	211	20	2	14	59	56	387
62	Garlic-Studded Kansas City Strip Loin	169	23	<1	8	42	61	445
62	Stuffed London Broil	296	37	3	15	45	90	171
63	Barbequed Flank Steak	560	29	27	38	60	68	2257
63	Grilled Porterhouse Steaks	357	38	1	21	55	107	576
64	Happy "Holla" Brandy Pepper Steak	226	27	<1	7	30	80	657
65	Fajitas on the Grill	246	27	18	5	20	84	1054
66	Kansas City Strip Steaks	1530	70	57	116	67	426	4310
67	Grilled Kansas City Strip Steaks	303	39	7	13	39	102	896
68	Rutherford's Black Jack "Drunk Steak"	362	40	4	13	33	102	801
69	Easy T-Bone Steaks	676	66	14	38	51	187	3924
69	Barbequed Beef Short Ribs	464	39	23	24	46	107	2153
70	Border Burgers	527	39	27	30	51	125	1173
71	Smoked Meat Loaf	281	25	6	17	55	92	164
71	Warm-You-Up Chili	281	24	34	6	19	43	1218
73	Bockwurst	136	12	1	9	63	51	358
74	Chorizo Sausage	205	11	1	17	77	48	298
75	Creole Pork Sausage	129	11	1	9	63	40	226
75	Hot Italian Pepper Sausage	129	11	<1	9	64	40	226
76	Hot Links	80	10	1	4	44	34	353
77	Happy "Holla" Barbequed Smoked Kielbasa	102	9	1	6	57	34	289
78	Polish Kielbasa	113	11	<1	7	59	38	351
79	Mr. T's Italian Sausage	78	10	<1	4	45	34	502

NUTRITIONAL PROFILES

Pg #	Recipe Title (Approx Per Serving)	Cal	Prot (g)	Carbo (g)	T Fat (g)	% Cal from Fat	Chol (mg)	Sod (mg)
79	Grilled Lamb Sausage	139	9	<1	11	71	38	689
80	Pistachio Sausage	142	12	1	10	65	40	298
81	Seafood Sausage	141	4	1	14	85	41	182
82	Barbequed Leg of Lamb	216	26	1	12	49	81	1087
83	BBQ Leg of Lamb[1]	442	27	17	31	62	92	291
84	Barbequed Leg of Lamb à la Dee's Diner	335	27	5	22	58	81	1160
84	Chinese-Style Lamb	197	27	4	7	35	85	270
85	Golden Heart Lamb	392	24	19	25	56	80	398
86	Honey-Grilled Shoulder of Lamb	224	23	9	10	40	79	240
86	Happy "Holla" Grilled Lamb Chops	157	15	2	10	56	44	262
87	Lamb Chops Jalapeño	298	19	35	10	29	62	919
88	Smoked Rack of Lamb	486	10	42	28	51	83	2903
89	Marinated Smoked Lamb Steak[1]	1989	6	4	220	98	21	16
89	Barbequed Denver Lamb Ribs	1471	87	1	122	76	396	1675
90	Hot Chinese Lamb Ribs	866	45	32	61	64	198	2365
91	Lamb Kabobs[1]	257	27	15	9	30	81	606
92	Rosemary-Marinated Lamb Kabobs[1]	258	24	26	7	24	65	1433
93	Thai Lamb Kabobs[1]	373	22	9	28	67	65	417
94	Lamb Burgers with Berry Sauce	524	40	10	36	62	150	580
95	Mesquite Grilled Amberjack	523	47	19	30	51	98	193
96	Lemon Grilled Catfish	372	36	1	24	59	157	925
96	State Championship Smoked Catfish	342	41	0	19	50	132	129
97	Monkfish with Jalapeños & Cilantro[1]	240	30	25	3	12	44	950
98	Grilled Halibut Tarragon	337	25	2	26	69	99	2429
98	BBQ Salmon	435	38	5	29	60	119	696
99	Smoked Salmon with Peppercorn Sauce[2]	1121	39	9	101	81	426	488
99	Grilled Salmon Steaks	689	50	39	37	49	205	303
100	Smoked Lake Trout[3]	272	42	0	11	36	125	2348
100	Trout with Lemon Zest Baste	412	29	7	30	65	148	306
101	Scallops-on-a-Stick[1]	234	23	8	11	44	43	263
102	Barbequed Shrimp	668	44	16	48	65	519	3026
102	Grilled Ginger Shrimp[1]	315	35	5	15	45	316	1394
103	Hot Peppered Shrimp[1]	310	35	7	15	45	316	1504
103	Mac's BBQ Shrimp	297	22	12	19	57	120	708
104	Spicy Golden Shrimp	116	11	7	5	38	74	1741
105	Uncle Beaver's Marinated Duck Breasts	477	36	7	33	62	133	1845
106	Barbequed Orange Duck	1126	54	6	97	78	269	1053
106	Smoked Duck[10]	860	49	0	72	77	214	6544

NUTRITIONAL PROFILES

Pg #	Recipe Title (Approx Per Serving)	Cal	Prot (g)	Carbo (g)	T Fat (g)	% Cal from Fat	Chol (mg)	Sod (mg)
107	Bobo Family Barbequed Rabbit	602	50	6	41	62	139	495
108	Grilled Rabbit	316	28	23	12	35	78	176
109	Barbequed Venison	532	42	18	33	55	150	2396
110	Grilled Deer Tenderloin	Nutritional profile for this recipe is not available.						
111	Grilled Venison Steak[1]	188	28	10	3	14	100	1418
111	Venison Burgers Italia	231	29	11	7	29	102	430
112	Beer Marinade[4]	336	<1	21	24	64	0	961
113	Burgundy Marinade[4]	245	1	11	8	28	0	210
113	Cider Mint Marinade[4]	160	<1	43	<1	1	0	1713
114	Dirty Dick's Poultry Marinade[4]	892	2	23	92	89	249	3076
114	Poultry Marinade[4]	1107	4	7	115	93	0	4111
115	Game Marinade[4]	59	1	17	<1	2	0	952
115	Lamb Marinade & Sauce[4]	366	1	4	27	65	0	2147
116	Oriental Hoisin Marinade[4]	561	5	125	<1	<1	0	7059
116	Pigskin Pete's Pork Marinade[4]	426	4	107	2	3	0	4505
117	Sesame Ginger Marinade[4]	1019	4	12	109	94	0	205
117	Teriyaki Marinade & Sauce[4]	471	6	19	43	79	0	6574
117	Vinaigrette Marinade[4]	1160	4	39	113	86	<1	2534
118	Barbeque Rub[5]	24	<1	6	<1	4	0	1857
118	Barbeque Beef Rub[5]	25	<1	6	<1	5	0	2053
119	Barbeque Poultry Rub[5]	28	<1	7	<1	5	0	1922
119	Barbeque Pork Rub[5]	22	<1	5	<1	9	0	1557
120	Barbeque Seasoning[5]	21	<1	5	<1	4	0	2558
120	Brown Sugar Rub[5]	29	<1	7	<1	3	0	2320
121	Crispy Critter Dry Rub & Basting Sauce[5]	15	1	3	<1	20	0	1674
121	Hot-Off-the-Grill Rub[5]	24	1	5	1	20	0	811
122	Hickory Barbeque Rub[5]	25	<1	6	<1	7	0	2139
122	K-Cass Dry Rub[5]	37	<1	9	<1	3	0	448
123	Kansas City Rib Rub[5]	27	<1	7	<1	7	0	1883
123	Powderpuff Rib Rub[5]	17	1	4	<1	12	0	2252
124	Spicy Barbecue Rub[5]	27	<1	6	<1	11	0	1550
124	TNT Rub[5]	36	<1	9	<1	4	0	1069
125	Apple City Sauce[6]	24	<1	6	<1	2	0	459
125	Barbeque Basting Sauce[6]	171	1	3	18	92	0	1543
126	Barbeque Sauce[6]	38	<1	5	2	47	0	295
126	Barbeque Dipping Sauce[6]	35	<1	9	<1	2	0	291
127	Hacking Sauce[6]*	29	<1	8	<1	1	0	258
127	Hot Pepper Basting Sauce[6]	72	1	8	5	55	0	2

NUTRITIONAL PROFILES

Pg #	Recipe Title (Approx Per Serving)	Cal	Prot (g)	Carbo (g)	T Fat (g)	% Cal from Fat	Chol (mg)	Sod (mg)
128	Kansas City Basting Sauce[6]	39	<1	7	1	29	0	277
129	Kansas City Classic Sauce[6]	50	<1	13	<1	3	0	306
130	Kentucky Colonel Sauce[6]	16	<1	2	1	54	3	298
131	Michael Conner's "Black Magic" Barbeque Sauce[6]	28	<1	6	1	19	0	175
131	Mop Sauce[6]	29	<1	1	2	73	0	205
132	Moppin' Sauce[6]	57	<1	<1	6	96	10	156
132	Basic Mopping Sauce[6]	41	<1	5	2	49	6	532
133	Wildman's Poultry Mop[6*]	96	<1	1	10	92	12	179
133	Mushroom Sauce for Steak[6]	107	1	1	11	92	38	9
134	Powderpuff Barbeque Sauce[6]	56	1	14	<1	4	0	298
134	Private Stock Steak Sauce[6]	260	1	2	26	89	71	469
135	Roasted Red Pepper Velvet[6]	191	1	1	21	97	13	177
136	Hot & Sweet Strawberry Barbeque Sauce[6]	30	<1	8	<1	3	0	192
137	Whiskeyque, Too Recipe[6]	41	<1	10	<1	2	0	525
137	Edsel Butter[6]	206	<1	1	23	98	62	110
138	Versatile Butter[6]	205	<1	<1	23	99	62	238
138	Honey Butter[6]	226	<1	6	23	89	62	239
138	Raspberry Butter[6]	215	<1	3	23	94	62	238
138	Orange Butter[6]	206	<1	<1	23	98	62	238
138	Barbeque Butter[6]	209	<1	1	23	97	62	281
138	Spicy Butter[6]	206	<1	<1	23	99	63	240
138	Nutty Butter[6]	230	1	1	26	97	62	238
140	Artichoke Dip	189	7	4	17	77	19	553
141	Potato Dip	53	<1	4	4	70	3	161
141	Texas Caviar	70	2	7	4	48	0	219
142	Pico de Gallo	39	1	4	3	54	0	4
142	Spicy Salsa	81	1	9	5	54	0	411
143	Hummus	191	3	14	14	65	0	436
143	Sausage Cheese Balls	57	2	3	4	58	9	142
144	Buffalo Wings	105	9	1	7	62	29	105
145	Nuclear Chicken Wings	106	9	1	7	59	29	983
145	Stuffed Morels	32	2	6	<1	9	<1	4
146	Marinated Mushrooms[1]	129	1	2	14	93	0	209
146	Grilled Oysters	67	2	3	5	69	8	43
147	Sausage Rolls	323	13	25	21	55	40	958
147	Hot Buttered Rum Mix	55	<1	6	4	59	10	2
148	Bean Salad	151	6	23	5	26	0	662
149	Southwest Bean Salad	305	10	30	17	48	13	699

NUTRITIONAL PROFILES

Pg #	Recipe Title (Approx Per Serving)	Cal	Prot (g)	Carbo (g)	T Fat (g)	% Cal from Fat	Chol (mg)	Sod (mg)
149	Brookville Coleslaw	152	1	18	9	51	33	235
150	Mississippi Delta Coleslaw	177	1	20	11	54	0	15
150	Dilled Potato Salad	291	2	20	23	70	16	540
151	German Potato Salad	332	3	31	23	60	0	129
152	Old Country Potato Salad	255	6	26	15	51	149	789
153	Texas Potato Salad[7]	294	2	23	22	66	13	198
153	Sauerkraut Salad	352	1	49	18	45	0	511
154	Curried Turkey & Wild Rice Salad	579	30	31	38	59	69	857
155	Grilled Vegetable Gazpacho	305	3	29	21	60	<1	691
156	Phantom of Memphis Gumbo	338	19	12	24	63	133	1363
157	Shrimp & Barbequed Sausage Gumbo	281	16	15	18	57	100	1181
158	Cowpoke Beans	482	30	84	5	9	5	969
159	Slow-Cooker Baked Beans	251	12	38	6	22	10	696
160	Glazed Carrots	75	1	10	4	46	10	109
160	Corn Casserole	450	11	43	28	54	112	1066
161	Parslied Corn in the Husk	186	3	20	13	56	31	131
161	Tex-Mex Barbequed Corn	173	3	19	11	53	28	472
162	Mushroom Casserole	412	10	24	32	68	107	938
163	Barbequed Vidalia Onions	150	1	6	13	74	31	121
163	Pickled Onions	213	1	34	9	37	0	1129
164	Peas & Garlic	150	6	20	6	34	0	133
164	Garlic New Potatoes	222	2	24	14	54	0	274
165	Grilled Cheese Potatoes	580	13	65	31	48	79	406
165	Twice-Baked Potatoes on the Grill	264	8	47	5	18	17	53
166	Fried Sweet Potatoes[8]	1013	1	14	108	94	0	6
166	Grilled Sweet Potatoes with Molasses Glaze	101	1	22	2	13	4	10
167	Sweet Potato Casserole	486	6	53	29	53	127	255
167	Grilled Vegetables	139	3	18	7	45	19	77
168	Margaritaville Veggies	124	2	10	8	50	0	1625
169	Stir-Fry Vegetables	33	2	6	<1	4	0	1156
170	Deviled Eggs	74	3	1	6	77	109	113
171	Grits Soufflé	316	11	16	23	66	198	694
172	Kickin' Hoppin' John[9]	290	21	47	3	9	7	151
172	Skillet Hopping John	278	10	48	5	16	10	1113
173	Mexican Rice Casserole	233	5	41	5	20	3	947
173	Wilder Than Wild Rice	317	10	62	3	8	0	295
174	Rosemary Apple Salsa	31	<1	6	1	32	0	60
174	Beer & Cheese Bread	207	6	28	7	32	20	495

NUTRITIONAL PROFILES

Pg #	Recipe Title (Approx Per Serving)	Cal	Prot (g)	Carbo (g)	T Fat (g)	% Cal from Fat	Chol (mg)	Sod (mg)
175	Bacon & Chili Corn Bread	182	5	28	6	29	29	592
175	Broccoli & Cheese Corn Bread	359	11	24	24	60	108	676
176	Grilled Stuffed Apples	274	2	54	6	18	8	36
177	Barbequed Bananas	253	1	44	10	32	25	102
178	Divine Cheesecake	509	9	47	33	57	171	369
179	Sausalito's Cheesecake	535	7	56	33	54	119	208
180	Gooey Butter Dessert	399	4	59	17	37	90	348
180	Homemade Vanilla Ice Cream	467	4	35	35	67	129	155
181	Strawberry Shortcake Royale	336	4	35	21	54	39	331
182	Frosted Brownies	163	2	26	7	35	36	67
183	Lemon Bars	132	2	19	6	39	37	69
183	White Chocolate Macadamia Cookies	148	1	15	9	56	21	114
184	Chocolate Chip Cookies	127	2	18	6	42	17	79
185	Chocolate-Chocolate Chip Cookies	210	3	24	14	54	31	70
186	Whoopie Pies	313	3	44	15	42	27	181
187	Apple Cake	324	3	44	16	43	42	68
187	Fresh Apple Cake with Caramel Icing	469	4	60	24	46	56	264
188	Carrot Cake	673	5	77	40	52	100	412
189	Whole Wheat Carrot Cake	578	8	70	33	48	133	519
190	Pumpkin Bundt Cake	443	4	59	22	44	69	237
191	Apple Cream Pie	974	10	122	53	47	102	651
192	Banana Caramel Pie	510	8	64	27	45	17	196
192	Million Dollar Pie	770	7	66	56	63	62	217
193	Peanut Butter Pie	426	9	55	20	41	96	289
194	Special Pie	745	8	85	44	51	214	272

[1]Nutritional profile includes entire amount of marinade.
[2]Nutritional profile includes entire amount of crème fraîche.
[3]Nutritional profile includes entire amount of soaking liquid.
[4]Nutritional profile based on serving size of 1 cup.
[5]Nutritional profile based on serving size of 1 tablespoon.
[6]Nutritional profile based on serving size of 1 ounce.
[7]Nutritional profile does not include pickle juice.
[8]Nutritional profile includes entire amount of peanut oil.
[9]Nutritional profile includes ham hock.
[10]Nutritional profile includes entire amount of rosemary mixture.
[*]Nutritional profile does not include cough syrup.
[†]Nutritional profile does not include barbeque rub.

Index

INDEX

INDEX

INDEX

INDEX

Kansas City Barbeque Society

Membership Form

For a meager $30.00 per year, you can be a part of the legendary KCBS family! This small fee entitles you to receive the world-renowned *KC Bullsheet*, which provides the most complete and up-to-date information on everything there is to know in the barbeque world, as well as a comprehensive, nation-wide listing of upcoming contests. Upon acceptance into the hallowed halls of KCBSdom, you will receive a membership certificate suitable for hanging in your garage or underneath your barbeque pit. What are you waiting for?

_____Yes! I want to become a member of the KCBS *TODAY!*

(Please print or write the following information carefully in order to avoid embarrassing misinterpretations!)

Name _____

Team Name _____

Address _____

City/State/Zip _____

Phone (Day) _____(Eve) _____

Referred by _____

Check all that apply:
   ❏ Contest Promoter ❏ Competition ❏ Novice ❏ Backyard ❏ Judge
   ❏ Writer ❏ Retailer ❏ Restaurateur ❏ Caterer ❏ Manufacturer

Method of payment:
   ❏ Check   Credit Card: ❏ VISA ❏ MasterCard ❏ American Express
   Card # _____
   Expiration Date _____

Please sign your name *as it appears on the card* but still legibly enough for us to read! _____

PLEASE READ CAREFULLY, CONSIDER MOMENTARILY AND SIGN BELOW: If selected for membership, I promise to faithfully uphold the tenets of a barbeque fanatic. I will cook and eat as much barbeque as the law allows. Signature _____

If you have questions before signing, call KCBS at (816) 765-5891 or fax us at (816) 765-5860. Out-of-state residents call (800) 963-KCBS.

Kansas City Barbeque Society
11514 Hickman Mills Drive
Kansas City, MO 64134

Kansas City Barbeque Society

Cookbook Order Form

Wow! This is such a great book, I want to send copies to all my friends!
Please send _____ copies of *The Kansas City Barbeque Society Cookbook:
Barbeque . . . it's not just for breakfast anymore* to me at:

Name _____

Address _____

City/State/Zip _____

Please send a copy to my friend at:

Name _____

Address _____

City/State/Zip _____

Message_____

Check, MasterCard/VISA, and American Express accepted.
Please add $4.00 shipping & handling per book.

Hardcover: $19.95 each x total number ordered _____ = _____
Special Notice!! KCBS Members Single Copy Price: $16.95
Shipping & Handling = _____
Total = _____

Softcover: $14.95 each x total number ordered _____ = _____
Special Notice!! KCBS Members Single Copy Price: $12.95
Shipping & Handling = _____
Total = _____

If paying by credit card, Expiration Date _____

Card #_____

Name AS IT APPEARS ON THE CARD_____

Mail your order and payment to: Kansas City Barbeque Society
11514 Hickman Mills Drive
Kansas City, MO 64134

OR phone or fax credit card orders to: (816) 765-5891
(816) 765-5860 fax

Thank you! And, now—fire up those grills!

Kansas City Barbeque Society
11514 Hickman Mills Drive
Kansas City, MO 64134